BEYOND
ANONYMITY

BEYOND ANONYMITY

A Commitment to a
Higher Consciousness

BY
Tammy Peacock McGahee

ISBN 0-9753057-0-0
Library of Congress PCN 2004092342

BOOK DESIGN BY Kelly Leavitt
COVER DESIGN BY Barry Foshee
AUTHOR PHOTO BY Joseph Craig Eggers

PUBLISHED BY
Truett Enterprises Press
P. O. Box 550160
Birmingham, AL 35255

DEDICATION

For my Mother,
who modeled unconditional love
long before I ever heard the term,
May I give to the world as lovingly and
as generously as you have given to me.
I love you a whole wide world full.

CONTENTS

1

ADDICTION AND RECOVERY—A NEW PERSPECTIVE 1

2

LIMITING BELIEFS 31

3

PREPARING FOR OUR ROLE 61

4

BRAVE ACTION 99

5

BECOMING THE PERSON YOU ARE MEANT TO BE 119

ACKNOWLEDGEMENTS

THERE ARE MANY PEOPLE TO THANK FOR THEIR SUPPORT during the years leading up to the publication of this book. For some, it was your ongoing support; for others, it was an encouraging word when this book was still a concept, a belief that this message needed to be published. Thanks to my husband, Ken, for your support and encouragement and for loving me like no one ever has. My friend and sister, Patsy—you are one of the greatest gifts in my life. Thanks to Ann White-Spunner, my constant companion on this journey, for supporting all my adventures. Jackie, my girlfriend across the pond, I am blessed to share another lifetime with you. My gratitude goes to Kelly Leavitt for guiding me through this process and making my message even clearer. To John and Jan Price, Lulu Richardson, John Austin, Ray Wooten, Savann Sherrill—your mere presence and occasional word have meant more than you could imagine. Two angels who asked to remain anonymous are like family to me, so I will just say to B and P, thank you for everything. And to all of my family members—Marshall, Steve, Phyllis, Sharon and Barbara, JC and Jerry—I love you all dearly. To all the friends in the fellowship, thank you for sharing this path with me, for helping me develop my strengths and loving me despite my shortcomings. And to everyone at Unity of Birmingham, thank you for being such a strong source of Love for me and our community.

PREFACE

LET ME BEGIN BY STATING THAT THIS BOOK IS WRITTEN IN compliance with the 12 Traditions and does not suggest anything that would encourage members to violate the Traditions. My decision to disclose that I am recovering, at the media level, is not a violation of the Traditions as long as I do not disclose affiliation with a particular fellowship. I am not a member of Alcoholics Anonymous nor do I speak for any fellowship. Nothing in this book is intended to suggest that the fellowships need changing in any way.

This book is not about making people in 12 Step communities special. Being special is about the ego. Recovery is about working to transcend the ego. This book speaks to a higher level of consciousness. It speaks *to* the recovering community *about* the recovering community. For those not in recovery who find this book, my hope is that you will gain a deeper understanding and respect of the potential for transformation that addiction holds for our society.

INTRODUCTION

THIS BOOK SPEAKS TO EVERY PERSON WHO IDENTIFIES HIM OR herself as being in recovery from any type of addiction, be it alcohol, drugs, food, work, sex, gambling, relationships, or any other compulsion. Being in recovery through a 12 Step program means several things. It means that we have recognized that, left to our own devices, we will continue to look for external resources to satisfy our internal yearnings. It also means we have committed to becoming productive members of society who live our lives based on spiritual principles. As recovering individuals, we have been assigned a role to play in this lifetime. Our addiction continues to prepare us for that role.

I am suggesting that perhaps we limit ourselves through the status quo that has developed of what successful recovery looks like. I am also suggesting that our second chance in life leaves us with a larger spiritual obligation to this world than we have previously acknowledged.

These ideas offer a new perspective on life that provides a deeper understanding of our interconnectedness. This new perspective is based on learning to live consciously, taking ownership of the world we live in.

I will refer to Alcoholics Anonymous (AA) frequently, not as a member or a representative of AA, but because it is the grandfather of the entire 12 Step movement.

I quote from several books, but of the 12 Step fellowships, only *Alcoholics Anonymous,* commonly known as the Big Book. While the other fellowships have developed significant literature for their specific areas, none has been able to capture the depth of inspiration found in *Alcoholics Anonymous.* As the foundation of the 12 Step movement, the early writings of AA envisioned the potential for millions of people to discover their spiritual path and recover from alcoholism. Alcoholics Anonymous established a set of concepts and principles that made its usefulness applicable across the board for millions of people. To create such a spiritual community in a manner that completely shielded it from outside influence was nothing short of a world wonder.

If we look at the history and evolution of Alcoholics Anonymous through the writings of Bill W., it has a lot to teach us about living consciously, using the challenges of life as stepping stones for positive change, while never underestimating the power that has been given us. One of the main concerns of Bill W. was that people would try to make the fellowship itself a cure-all for the problems of society. While the fellowships were never intended to solve the problems of the world, they may in fact be preparing their members to accept this responsibility.

Much soul searching has gone into the creation of this book and my desire to avoid conflict has delayed the project extensively. For me, the negative consequences of not writing this book became greater than the potential conflict that might arise from writing it. New ideas are often difficult to embrace. Where the fellowship or recovery is concerned, we tend to become defensive and often discount new ideas with contempt. I recognize the controversial nature of this book and hope that you will explore these ideas with all the honesty, open-mindedness and willingness you used in early recovery.

1
ADDICTION AND RECOVERY

A New Perspective

Cowardice asks the question—is it safe?
Expediency asks the question—is it politic?
Vanity asks the question—is it popular?
But conscience asks the question—is it right?
And there comes a time when one must take
a position that is neither safe, not politic, nor popular;
but one must take it because it is right.

—DR. MARTIN LUTHER KING, JR.

No one knows better than the recovering community the pervasiveness of addiction in our society. Addictions to food, drugs, alcohol, gambling, relationships, spending, work and sex, to name a few, are interwoven in all aspects of our society. Addiction has reached epidemic proportions and increases daily. It is so common in American culture that we, as a society, are becoming desensitized to it. The consequences of addiction are so extensive there is no way to truly calculate the financial cost to our society. Despite the fact that addiction costs taxpayers billions of dollars each year, our greatest minds have been unable to find an effective solution to deal with this social issue and its symptoms. However, small groups of individuals located throughout the world have a solution for the individual who is ready and willing to move beyond active addiction. We know the solution from first-hand experience. We live it every day.

But is our experience with this solution preparing us for a larger role in society? What if, from a soul perspective, addiction and recovery are preparing us to play a major role in the transformation of our world, a role that includes but far exceeds helping other addicts to recover? There are signs all around you that indicate that you have a purpose much higher than just staying sober or abstaining from your addictive behavior.

When the founders of Alcoholics Anonymous, the grandfather of the 12 Step movement, adopted the slogan, "When anyone, anywhere reaches out for help, I want the hand of AA to be there and for that I am responsible," they made their intention very clear. They didn't say when *any alcoholic* reaches out, they said when *anyone* reaches out. This is a broad and powerful commitment. While not all of the fellowships have adopted this slogan, it clearly defines the role that the founding members of AA envisioned for the recovering individual.

By laying the groundwork for all the fellowships that would later develop, AA did in fact establish a path to prepare individuals for playing a role in transforming the world, a role that far exceeds our current understanding of helping other addicts. Recovery is preparing us, individually and collectively, to become even more responsible members of society, to take ownership of our world in the same way we take ownership of the fellowship, to expand our commitment that "our common welfare should come first," to encompass not just members of the fellowship or those who are addicted, but society as a whole. Addiction is a blessing in disguise for society, just as it is for the individual.

Members of the fellowships have often wondered whether the founders, Bill Wilson or Dr. Bob Smith, truly recognized the impact the fellowships would have in transforming our world. Sure, they knew they had tapped into something that would transform alcoholics, but did they recognize the influence millions of recovering people could have in shaping public policy, protecting our environment, defending human rights and further transforming our world?

We have learned that addiction is a spiritual issue. We must ask ourselves if the same holds true for society. Is the ever-growing pervasiveness of addiction an indication of an enormous spiritual revolution building in our society? Are the millions of people addicted to food, drugs, alcohol, sex, work, gambling, spending and relationships experiencing the spiritual hunger that once consumed us? Are their souls using addiction as a vehicle to move them to their spiritual path? Can you imagine how different our world would be if the millions who are currently addicted in one form or another were to step onto their spiritual path? And what if they went beyond the current status quo of successful recovery—what if they decided to move beyond their individual lives and make a conscious commitment to transform our world?

Virtually every segment of society is dealing with chronic social issues which plague our society—issues ranging from inadequate education to lack of medical care, from overcrowding in prisons to abuse of the environment, from domestic violence to homelessness, and from AIDS to government and corporate fraud. Just as recovery from addiction requires action, a willingness to go to any lengths, transformation in society requires a consistent organized effort by its citizens.

Recovery has taught us that the solution—one which can be applied to more conditions than just active addiction—is a way of life that reflects a constantly evolving understanding of universal truths and higher consciousness. As we expand our understanding of the role addiction is playing within society, not only will we be able to address the underlying issues, but we will intuitively understand how to be of greatest service.

Addiction will continue to thrive until society shifts its understanding of this issue. Individuals in recovery can facilitate this shift in perception by helping society understand that addiction is a symptom of a deeper issue. We are in a position to make a unique contribution to society. We have already, individually and collectively, gone through the process of identifying the deeper issue, using spiritual principles as a solution.

There are many reasons for us to become more involved at a societal level. The main reason is that we do not want to sit back and watch the deterioration of our quality of life. As long as we, as a society, focus on the problem, we give it energy, which means it will continue to grow. It is our tax dollars that are being using to fight a war on drugs, a war that we cannot win based on the current perspective. It is our tax dollars that are being used to build more prisons and incarcerate the addicted. It is our tax dollars that are being wasted in bureaucratic spending. It is our responsibility to ensure that our children are properly educated. Just as spiritual solutions are necessary for the individual, spiritual solutions are necessary for our society.

Too often, we as a society allow logic and personal gain to tilt the scales in the decision-making process. As a society, we think that if we funnel more money into an issue, we are addressing the issue. More money is not the solution to the issues faced by our society. Just as the individual must thoroughly inventory their life in order to recover, so must we as a society identify the causes and conditions that set these patterns in motion. Who is more qualified to begin this process than the recovering community? While it may still take years for society to embrace a new perspective on addiction, it is our responsibility to spearhead this social effort.

The recovering individual has many skills that make him or her qualified to move into a more prominent role in transforming our society. We are already present at every level of society, tucked away in communities throughout most of the world. Our familiarity with not fitting in supports our going against the norms of society as we embrace what many will perceive to be civil disobedience. There are already millions of recovering individuals across the globe. If you look at the growth of the 12 Step movement over the last fifty years and project even fifty percent growth over the next fifty years, the recovering community will be enormous. Raising the status quo of successful recovery and redefining what it means to be of maximum service benefits everyone.

Your exact role as a member of society depends upon your circumstances and where you are in your own personal recovery. Personal recovery must come first. However, many of us will need to take a higher profile and acknowledge that personal recovery is an aspect of who we are. We have to move beyond our fears and the repercussions of acknowledging our addiction in order to remove the stigma that society has placed on addiction. The stigma surrounding addiction blocks the growth of the individual, as well as society. Allowing the stigma to remain is to perpetuate the myth that addiction is a moral issue with which only a few are afflicted. After all, you would be hard pressed to find a family not directly touched by some form of addiction, especially considering the prevalence of obesity and spending in our society.

Our society is at a crossroads. Just as we found ourselves there individually, we are now there collectively. We have the same choice that was presented to us in *Alcoholics Anonymous*—"to go on to the bitter end blotting out the consciousness of our intolerable situation or to pick up the simple kit of spiritual tools that have been laid at our feet." You may think that our society has not yet reached the point of being intolerable, since we still have freedom and many luxuries. However, we also see greed, envy, pride, gluttony, anger, and lust manifesting in everyday life. These form the crux of the issue. Not only do we see the presence of these shortcomings, we sometimes argue more strongly for our right to exercise these qualities than we do for love, peace and tolerance. Just as we tell the newcomer that they don't have to hit the lowest bottom possible, so must we look at what type of "bottom" we are willing to allow our society to reach.

In order to move beyond the current status quo of successful recovery, the recovering person must begin to look at addiction and its relationship to society from a higher perspective. Carl Jung believed that addiction is a thirst for wholeness. Wholeness encompasses all aspects of life and humanity as one unit, not divided by time, knowledge or physical location. Many philosophers have speculated that addiction is the soul's way of overcoming the perceived separation from the Divine Presence. If this is true, then what is happening to all of the people in this world who are actively addicted to drugs, sex, relationships, food, shopping, and gambling? Are they searching for the Divine through external sources? Their soul is moving them in this direction for a reason. Is the epidemic of addiction symbolic of our society's search for wholeness? Just as your challenges are present to take you to a higher consciousness, so are the challenges of our society present to move us collectively to a higher level of consciousness.

Is it such a stretch of the imagination to believe that the same solutions that work for the individual will also work for society? Not if you are familiar with 12 Step programs. We see miracles occur every day. We must shift our perspective of service to encompass the relationship between our individual choices, our community and the world as a whole. We already do this within the fellowship by considering our choices in relationship to the fellowship as a whole.

Addiction and recovery are preparing us to move into a more prominent role in the transformation of our society. Acceptance of this role may initially appear to go against what you have been taught in your respective fellowships. Remember, the goal of recovery is to be of greatest service to God and our fellow man. I ask that you look closely at the ideas presented in these pages with all the open-mindedness available to you, to find your own truth. In order to take a more active role in the transformation of our world, you will have to explore your limiting beliefs about yourself, as well as about the fellowship. You will need to embrace a deeper understanding of how life is preparing you for your role, to shift from living one day at a time to living consciously in each moment. And most importantly, you will have to take brave action. We as recovering individuals can remove the stigma that is attached to addiction. However, this will require that we become much more proactive and responsible within our respective communities.

Collective Consciousness

What is the use of a house if you haven't
got a tolerable planet to put it on?

—HENRY DAVID THOREAU

THE COLLECTIVE CONSCIOUSNESS OF A SOCIETY REFLECTS THE personalities, prejudices, sensitivities, values, and consciousness of its individual members. It reflects the challenges most prevalent among individual members of society. It is clearly evident among the leaders and the issues of that society. The collective consciousness of the United States has elected alcoholics/addicts to their highest office. Our last two presidents would meet all the diagnostic criteria for dependency. During both administrations, we have seen how untreated addiction has the propensity to yield destruction—emotionally, spiritually and financially. If our leaders reflect the consciousness of the public, what does this reveal about our society and where we are with addiction? It tells me that addiction has become a leading issue. It tells me that the addicted are everywhere, that everyone in our society is touched by addiction, either directly or indirectly. Our resistance to dealing with the issue indicates that we are still more concerned with appearances than with spiritual growth. It also tells me that as a society we have not yet learned the practical application of spiritual principles on a daily basis. We are spiritually unbalanced.

The prevalence of addiction itself indicates that, as a society, we must search externally for something to quell an inner yearning, that we must control and manipulate in order to maintain a sense of power. It indicates that, as a society, we do not have the skills to appropriately deal with conflict, or to even recognize every individual's value as a human being. An emergence of a tremendous spiritual energy of healing, however, is seeking to manifest in our world—an emergence that we, as members of the recovering community, are well qualified to support and nurture.

It is time that we begin a national discussion about our values. Regardless of what we profess them to be, our choices reveal what we really hold as valuable. For instance, our entire future rests in the hands of our children, yet we disregard the importance of their education and the many issues they face during adolescence. We send our kids to schools that are not properly funded, to sit in classrooms that are overcrowded. We allow their diets to consist of junk food filled with food additives. We medicate them to control their behavior, and expect them to learn. We spend more time debating whether to educate teenagers about birth control than we do about how to provide them with alternatives that validate their personal worth in ways other than being sexually active.

For decades, kids have been flocking to gangs in their

search for a sense of belonging because our society has been unable to offer them another option to fulfill their needs. Kids are selling drugs because they see it as their best option for getting ahead and moving up in the world. Even when they know the odds are against them, they risk their lives and their freedom because they perceive the risk to be worth it. We cannot afford to look for someone to blame for these conditions. Whether or not parents should be able to deal with the issues of their children is irrelevant. After all, we are talking about our choices, our values and our future. The choices made by the government, who are elected by the citizens, reflect the values of the collective conscience.

Many of our choices indicate that we value wealth and power, which are just as addictive as any tangible substance. They may have even more power for destruction among society. The future of thousands of families is being threatened by executives whose greed is bankrupting corporations. Huge corporations are influencing public policy concerning our environment, pretending that their motives are in the best interest of the people rather than their profit margin. The public is constantly challenged with finding reliable information and discerning who is trustworthy among corporations, politicians and the media.

We have become a gambling society in the race, not to keep up with the Jones, but to exceed them. Along the way, we sacrifice not just our children, but also our forests, our water supply, our air, our stability, and any culture that stands in the way of progress or financial gain. We suppress technological and medical advances that would allow humanity to evolve more quickly. Instead, we support technology that allows us to genetically engineer our food supply in order to increase profits. With all the technological advances in the last century, is it possible that we can't find a cure for cancer? Have you ever stopped to consider how many people are becoming wealthy by ensuring that cancer continues to exist? As a society, are we more concerned with profits than the toxins in the air and the water? And what about our automobiles? Why aren't we mass-producing vehicles that meet the needs of the consumer while being environmentally friendly? What does this reveal about the collective consciousness?

We see violence escalating within our communities and at the world level. We live in a world where acts of terrorism are being met with war. We allow our fear to dictate our choices, to override basic human rights in the name of homeland security. As a nation, we recognized the error of detaining individuals of Japanese descent after Pearl Harbor was bombed. Yet, since 9/11, we have detained thousands of individuals of Middle Eastern descent at Guantanamo Bay. As a society, we have to ask to ourselves if the choices we are making are really indicative of a civilized society. Or do they more clearly show evidence of a self-centered society? The hallmark of all addiction is self-centeredness. It doesn't matter if we have found a way to manipulate the facts in order to make our choices legal. We are a world leader; our choices, social policy and commitment to human rights should reflect this. Do society's choices reflect the spiritually-based principles by which you as a recovering person live?

There are many correlations between the individual who is addicted and the society that is addicted. Both are experiencing an incongruence of values; both are attempting to use external sources to heal an internal yearning. Both generally have ideals for a higher moral standard by which to live. Both are spiritually, emotionally and sometimes financially bankrupt. Both use denial to avoid acknowledging painful aspects of their identity. Both are intrinsically self-centered. Both think the world revolves around them. Both want to avoid the issue of addiction completely.

Just as the recovering individual had to acknowledge that there was a problem, so must we acknowledge that there are serious issues facing our society. We must also acknowledge the insanity of continuing to address these issues as we have in the past. The normal channels to solve these issues have been ineffective because we have not gotten to the deeper issue. The challenges of our society reveal the discrepancy of values held by the majority of individuals in our society. The discrepancy of the average citizen transfers into an incongruity in the collective consciousness. Using education as an example, do individuals without children see it as a priority? And what about the millions of people who have gotten by without a college degree? Do they consider education a priority? How many citizens without school-age children attend school board meetings? Does your average elementary or high school have any type of activity or organization equivalent to the PTA, which seeks to include individuals without children in their support system?

As a democratic society, the choices made by our government reflect the consciousness of a critical mass. Our behavior indicates that we value our automobiles more than our air quality, that profit is more important than our earth, that education is not a priority for every person, whether they are a child or an adult. The fear that gripped the United States after the terrorist attacks on 9/11 is manifesting in our foreign policy, our economy and our government. There is an insidious sense of insecurity and distrust among the American public, a need to react in a way to reestablish our sense of safety, control and personal power. Americans pulled together after the attacks in a way that had not occurred since the Depression. A resurgence of patriotism was evident everywhere. We moved through the stages of grief together, recognizing that we have stepped into a new era and can never go back to the pre-9/11 reality of our world. With this recognition came a deeper uncertainty of the future. Many individuals took financial control by taking their money out of the stock market and moving it into more stable and reliable investments. They limited their spending and cancelled trips. Businesses began to scale down, terminating their employees. Some even closed their doors.

Our government reflected this sense of distrust, lack of control and insecurity. We declared that other nations were a threat to national security and exerted our authority and power through military action—acts that allowed us to briefly recapture a sense of control and power. We questioned other nations that did not agree with our decisions, revealing our distrust of both their motives and their commitment to America. While in a state of shock, the government enacted laws that certainly border on violating civil rights. Attempts to revive the economy resulted in many individuals, as well as the nation, going deeper into debt. Our government manipulated the citizens, the economy and the decision-making process in order to regain a sense of power and control. Do you see unmanageability anywhere in this picture?

As you consider this thought, I ask you to be open to new levels of truth. According to Dr. David Hawkins, whose study of consciousness is detailed in his book, *Power vs. Force,* there are many forms of truth. He states that individual truth is influenced by a number of factors, but primarily the individual's ability to conceptualize, their level of intellect and their consciousness. For information to be true, it must have meaning and fit into your frame of reference. Your personal truth is the foundation for how you choose to live and a determinant of your behavior. This means that we must be willing to acknowledge that, while a concept or an ideal may be one's personal truth, it is not necessarily true for everyone. As your consciousness evolves, your concepts of truth will also evolve. A good example of this can be seen in the contrast of seasoned members and individuals early in recovery. Their reality and understanding of what is true are often polar opposites. Newcomers may enter the fellowship with no concept of a Higher Power, yet their reality changes as they begin to apply spiritual principles in their daily lives and increase their understanding of a Higher Power. As you grow in your knowledge, understanding and awareness of a Higher Power, you raise the collective consciousness.

You and millions of other recovering individuals are an important part of the solution for transforming our world. When you understand the relationship between individual and collective consciousness, you will see why every single individual doing their part is crucial to creating the world we want to live in.

So, how do you contribute to the consciousness of our society? You make a positive contribution by continuing to grow spiritually, constantly striving to attain your highest potential, and practicing prayer and meditation. There is a tendency to practice prayer and meditation just enough to maintain your spiritual connection. This is one of those points where you will need to move beyond the current status quo. Your inner guidance will reveal more about the specifics of your contribution to society, however your commitment to prayer and meditation is equally as important as the work you choose to do. We must always be aware that our consciousness is revealed in our choices and our behavior.

Everywhere you turn there are opportunities to be of service to our society: being active with your favorite charity, working to save our environment, protecting animals, providing for the less fortunate, being informed about the actions of your elected officials, voting, writing letters, campaigning for candidates whose values reflect yours, forming grass roots organizations to work for a good cause, recycling, financially supporting your favorite causes, mentoring or simply being kind to the kid in the grocery store. Every step you take to release your emotional baggage allows you to show more love and compassion, which will be reflected in the consciousness of our society. Every gesture made from your most conscious place, even those you may think are insignificant, will have a positive influence in our world. While you may be skeptical that raising your personal consciousness will be reflected in society, certainly you can see how a million people raising their consciousness across the world will elevate the collective consciousness.

The entire world is experiencing an integration of knowledge that reflects a higher consciousness. However, we have to do more. The gift of recovery charges us with the responsibility to care for our fellow man, not just others who are addicted. The time has come for individuals in recovery to commit to moving beyond the current status quo of successful recovery. To be effective in using the tools of recovery at a societal level, we must allow ourselves to see the bigger picture and understand our interconnectedness. We must look at life from a broader perspective, to acknowledge and discuss the parallels between our individual lives and society as a whole.

Why Us?

The ultimate measure of a man is not
where he stands in moments of comfort
and convenience but where he stands
at times of challenge and controversy.

—MARTIN LUTHER KING, JR.

IT WILL TAKE A GRASS ROOTS EFFORT BY A LARGE GROUP TO shift the direction our society has been taking. I am not suggesting that the recovering community per se become the grass roots organization that takes on this challenge. However, I am suggesting that many of us are in recovery at this moment to play a role in this process. During active addiction, many of us came close to death many times, but we survived, often becoming aware that we had some purpose for being here that we had not yet fulfilled. Not only have we been given a second chance, many of us have been given a life more blessed than we could ever have imagined.

What will bring about peace in our world and respect for our planet? There is no simple answer to that question, but we hold tremendous power when we accept responsibility. No place is this power more evident than in our commitment to protecting the fellowships. Every member of a 12 Step fellowship has seen a newcomer confronted when they dishonored the group in some way. This is because the members have assumed ownership of the respective fellowships. Twelve Step fellowships can only be destroyed from within, therefore members respond strongly to disrespect or a violation of the Traditions. As long as a fellowship operates within the 12 Traditions, nothing in this world can harm them. The members understand the spiritual power that is inherent in the 12 Steps and the 12 Traditions and accept responsibility to ensure their perpetual existence. Should we as responsible members of society respond as strongly when we see individuals disrespecting our society or our earth?

What stops us from holding this same allegiance and commitment to our respective communities, our fellow man, and our planet? Only a shift in perspective stands in the way. Many will say, "I can't be responsible for the whole world," but if you don't adopt a portion of this responsibility, who will? We all have to be responsible for this world. When world peace occurs, it will, in large part, be a result of the collective effort of individuals to accept responsibility for their fellow man and apply spiritual principles on a global basis, using many of the same principles we have *already learned* in the fellowships. Our experience makes us uniquely prepared to play a major role in accepting responsibility for creating the world we want to live in.

The recovering community has an established structure for making choices through spiritually-based principles—the 12 Steps and the 12 Traditions. Millions of people in recovery—in every profession, on every continent—make choices on a daily basis that have the potential to directly influence everything from public policy on worldwide issues to the status quo within our communities. We have tapped into a power so strong that it, when focused, has the potential to raise the consciousness of society tremendously. All it will take for us to play a more active role in the transformation of our world is for each recovering person to decide that the evolution and the existence of this world depends on their small but vital contribution.

Our experience with addiction and recovery has taught us many lessons that the world has yet to integrate. We understand that addiction is a symptom of a deeper issue, that in order to maintain our recovery we must continue to grow spiritually and to be of service to others. We have seen how the experience of active addiction can be tremendously useful in our recovery. It allowed us to own shadow aspects of ourselves that most people prefer to deny they possess. It taught us a level of compassion for our fellow man that only experience with despair can provide.

The founding principles of the 12 Steps come from ancient spiritual traditions, so it should not be surprising that they are designed to take us to extraordinary places, to help us become extraordinary beings. The 12 Step fellowships have given us tools that allow us to model exceptional skills many people have not yet learned—skills such as knowing how to peacefully coexist with others, regardless of their spiritual practices, and promptly making amends when we are wrong or have made choices that were in some way harmful. We have been taught to place "principles before personalities," to refrain from holding resentments or seeking revenge. When in conflict, we understand the importance of looking at *our* part in whatever situation we find ourselves in, rather than blaming others. We understand that we may continue to fall short of our stated goals for living a spiritual life, but we have a formula that allows us to learn from our challenges and refocus on our path. Granted, we have learned many of these lessons the hard way (and often it was not a pretty sight), but every day we teach others new to the fellowship how to do this—by our example.

All behavior serves a purpose, however everyone does not choose to explore that purpose or how it serves him or her. In recovery, we are taught to continuously examine our motives, to dig deeper into the causes and conditions that established the patterns in our life. This ongoing self-examination allows us to reach for spiritual solutions to even the most complex situations in life. Just as we used the principles and tools of 12 Step fellowships for our individual recovery, we must begin to apply these same tools and perspective on a more global level.

As a society, we say that we value diversity and proclaim,

"In God We Trust," however our behavior indicates that we place more faith in science and intellect than we do in spiritual practices. In placing our faith in science and technology, we are essentially telling the next generation that spiritual solutions are limited in their usefulness and that miracles are something for the chosen. Do you see anything wrong with this picture? As a recovering person, you know from experience that our planet will not survive with this attitude. Sure, there is a place for science and technology, but spiritual solutions are vital for the highest evolution of the human race. Without a spiritual solution, how many of us would even be alive? Many of us would be dead by now if our reliance had been primarily on people and intellect.

The fellowships have offered a safe haven for millions of people, a place where they feel like they belong and are accepted for who they are. For many, it is the first experience of ever having fit in anywhere. We need to acknowledge that while fitting in can be comforting, it can also be constraining. Have you ever considered that maybe there is a purpose for your feeling like you don't fit in among society? Is it possible that your discomfort is there to stimulate you to become a source of change for your community, rather than trying to change yourself so that you fit in with the dysfunction that is rampant in our world?

Your resistance to conforming to many of the expectations of society may actually be your strength rather than your shortcoming. That rebellious nature can be shaped and channeled into productive avenues. Feeling as though you fit in is important for many people because it represses the fear of being alone. Adopting a more prominent role in the transformation of society may force you to work through fears that go to the core of your being. If so, then know they are a blessing in disguise.

Addicts tend to perceive themselves as being different. In some respects, we do seem to have a particular mental twist to the way our mind works and our outlook on life. However, I urge you to use extreme caution in seeing yourself as different. Some people see different as good, others see it as bad. Either way, it is a judgment of yourself and can be a way that your ego is setting you up to maintain comfort in your own dysfunction and denial. The difference can be beneficial if used to prepare yourself to walk a path outside the conventions of society. You see, we are accustomed to being outside the norm. You have always walked to a different beat. Even if you never knew it before, the different beat was there for a reason. Perhaps your purpose in life is to use this difference to stand among your peers and question the sanity of what our society is creating. Most people in recovery have known some form of hell and can recognize when they are skirting that edge again. This familiarity with conflict and internal struggle makes us uniquely prepared to go the distance that will be required to create the social changes that are needed in our society. We know at the depth of our souls that our personal solutions will always involve more spiritual growth. Why wouldn't this also be the solution to the challenges that face our society?

While we have been conditioned to accept certain situations, believe what we are told, blend in with our community and behave according to what society has deemed the norm, for most addicts, the conditioning was never completely successful. Throughout history, we have seen how governments, religions and other institutions felt the common people could not be trusted to make good decisions and needed to be guided and protected. Unfortunately, we see some of this in the fellowships as well. The problem with this approach is that it promotes dependence and mediocrity rather than encouraging creativity and ingenuity. It shifts our dependence from a Higher Power to people and institutions. It is time to challenge certain misguided beliefs established for reasons involving control, power or monetary gain. Individually and collectively, we must allow the presence of a Higher Power to truly manifest in all of our affairs.

Our society will be set on the path to recovery by uncommon action taken by presumably common people—people like you and me. Many of the challenges faced by society will be remedied without government intervention when enough citizens allow their creativity and passion to be channeled into social solutions. While many people are already living their dreams, when a fraction of the millions of recovering individuals allow themselves, as well, to achieve their highest potential, we will see a remarkable difference in our society. The idea you have always had to start an innovative program to mentor kids may profoundly influence hundreds of lives, or the book you have dreamed of writing may motivate others to also live their dreams.

Unfortunately, many within the recovering community are so busy trying to fit in that they quash any idea that might take them further from the mainstream. We often hear of people who, though successful in recovery, remain unfulfilled, and use lack of time and money as reasons for not following their passion. As a recovering person, you know that your needs will always be met. Your soul recognizes the greatest good for all concerned and uses your dreams as just one of the ways it seeks expression.

In the last twenty years, we have witnessed an explosion in the 12 Step movement, as it now encompasses virtually every pathological behavior. There is a reason millions of people are being led to their spiritual path through 12 Step fellowships. Whether it is the balancing of a karmic debt or part of the spiritual evolution of our world, we must keep our eyes on the bigger picture. Personal recovery will be a small comfort if we stand by and allow society and our environment to deteriorate. Your willingness to receive clarity about your role in the transformation of our world is all that you need to begin. If you view life as though the survival of this world depends on your developing to your highest potential, then you will be used for just that purpose. It is crucial that each person does what he or she can with the power they have. This will require that a lot of us make a decision to be seen and heard, to commit once again to going to an even higher level of spiritual growth, to really being of *maximum service* to our world. It will require that you make the same commitments to the world that you made to yourself and the fellowship when you decided to enter recovery.

2
LIMITING
BELIEFS

The surest way to corrupt a youth is to instruct him
to hold in higher esteem those who think alike

than those who think differently.

—FRIEDRICH NIETZSCHE

HOPEFULLY, THIS DIALOGUE WILL STIMULATE YOU TO LOOK AT the tough issues that surround you every day, and to examine your responsibility to be a part of the solution. We must continue to penetrate our denial. Honesty is not just telling the truth; it means "without deceit," which covers the areas of omission and manipulation. At some point in recovery, everyone faces the question of whether honesty is always the best policy. Beliefs that limit our willingness to participate in life, to become agents of change within the fellowship and society, keep us locked into a status quo of successful recovery that we must surpass in order to reach our highest potential. We do ourselves as well as our fellow man a disservice when we are unwilling to face our denial.

There are many terms to describe the chatter in your head, but mainly they are just lies that you tell yourself. You may tell yourself that it's okay to be financially irresponsible, to be misleading at times in your daily interactions, that you can't afford to give to charities, that your relationships are healthy, that you can't leave your job even if you are unhappy, that you are not angry, that it's not your job to keep up with what is going on in your community or the world, that you don't have time to volunteer, that there is nothing you can do to create change in our world. The list can be endless. There is always a tendency to justify why you need to maintain your denial about things. This is the very nature of denial itself.

Denial allows you to avoid responsibility. Yet, denial of what is really going on within you is basically untreated addiction, which eventually leads the recovering person to swap additions, even though the new addiction may be less obvious and sometimes less destructive. Consequences for denial often manifest in the form of struggle, lack and/or discontent, which are the Divine's way of saying it is time to break through your denial about some aspect of yourself that needs to be addressed in order for you to be of greater service. It is the soul seeking higher expression. There is an evolution to our consciousness; we don't just wake up enlightened. Penetrating the denial to master our soul lessons is not optional if we want to experience our highest potential.

As you grow to higher levels of understanding about your purpose in this world and why your soul manifested addiction in this lifetime, you may experience the feelings and conflicts that initiated your addiction. They may surface in a more subtle way, but they are essentially the same. This is a time to be extremely cautious about relapsing and/or swapping addictions. Remember that the substance, person or behavior of active addiction was only a symptom of a deeper issue. As feelings and conflicts resurface, they indicate a readiness to move to deeper levels of knowledge, understanding, and awareness of spiritual principles. They indicate a need for more clearing of emotional baggage.

Regardless of what you have accomplished in recovery or how long you have been recovering, you still have unresolved issues that will surface when you go beyond the safety of your world. In order to maintain a sense of personal safety and control, we often avoid people, places and things that might arouse any fear or sense of discomfort. The aspects of ourselves that we choose to deny are those which we often judge most harshly in others. The aspects of ourselves that we seek to avoid are those we avoid in others. The people and circumstances we avoid are just as revealing as the situations and people with whom we interact, because they show us where we still need to heal.

Many individuals in recovery become active with groups and causes that reflect the wounds they are attempting to heal. For instance, an individual who was abused as a child might choose a position working with individuals who are dealing with abuse issues. However, this same individual may avoid working with the perpetrators of abuse. The avoidance of perpetrators reveals the unhealed aspects of their wound and holds the potential to develop even greater strengths. While we might find the perpetrator's behavior incomprehensible, surely the recovering individual recognizes the need for everyone to be given the opportunity to change, to receive support from the community. How many of us would be in recovery without the strong support system that showed us compassion, regardless of our past?

Another example is the case of Jill, a thirty-year-old executive who grew up in poverty. She worked hard to move beyond the socioeconomic status in which she was raised. Jill excelled in college and has a successful career. She is active in the arts community and supports the local animal shelter. Both charities allow her to make valuable contributions to society, while maintaining her sense of safety and control within her belief system. Because of own her determination, Jill has found it very difficult to interact and empathize with women who are unable, for various reasons, to achieve a better life for themselves. Although she is not consciously aware of it, Jill identifies personal value with social status; in fact, her entire identity is built on it. By avoiding women of lower socioeconomic status, Jill is able to maintain a belief that she is in some way superior to them. Instead of clarifying her values or recognizing the lessons inherent in her early challenges, she has sought to deny that aspect of her life. She found poverty repulsive and believes that determination will allow anyone to move ahead in life. Whether she is right isn't the issue. Jill is unable to see how many people have supported her ambition and her progress, nor can she recognize how beneficial she might be in supporting the ambition of other women. Instead, she judges their situation. Overall, Jill is a compassionate person who is committed to social causes; she is, however, totally unaware of the incongruence in her stated values and her identity.

Is Jill really living her life to its fullest? Not if she avoids situations and people that might challenge her belief system. Just as a structure built on an unstable foundation will not endure, an identity built of conflicting beliefs will have to shift in some form. Life will present you with opportunities to clarify your values as you develop to your highest potential. Before every major breakthrough or shift in consciousness, it will be necessary for you to penetrate your denial at a deeper level. We have to be willing to look at the choices we make, as well as those we avoid.

Have you looked at the limits you place on your relationship with the God of your understanding? If the God of your understanding is always with you, it implies that this power is within you and/or surrounds you. What is it that scares us about an intimate relationship with the Creator? Why do we tend to keep it in the authoritarian role rather than making it our best friend and constant companion? Why does the thought of being able to tap into this unlimited power at all times frighten us? Why don't we constantly hear the voice of the God within us, rather than believing that this gift is only available to a chosen few? Why does society label people who can hear this voice as crazy? If we all need each other and we know it, then why do we act as if world issues aren't our problem? Why do we (who know better) sit back, while society makes one set of spiritual beliefs right and another wrong?

Don't they all hold common threads? If we acknowledge that they do have common core beliefs, does that undermine any particular faith?

The whole concept that we are one with our Creator scares us so much because it lays at our feet a tremendous responsibility—one that we are meant to share and use to create the quality of life that we want in our world. Marianne Williamson has said that we can expect God to take a wrecking ball to our life when we commit totally to a spiritual way of life. Perhaps this is because of all the fallacies that make up our reality, or maybe it is the best way to completely get our attention. Either way, it is often a necessary part of spiritual growth.

Your expectations of life itself can hold tremendous insight into the beliefs that limit or delay your spiritual development. In early recovery, I thought if I did my best to apply the principles of the fellowship in my daily life, everything would be okay, that my life would be relatively free of conflict. With the tools I gained in recovery, I thought I could respond well to most any situation that came my way. My expectation was based on several false premises: that I actually could practice the principles in all my affairs on a daily basis; that life is supposed to be fair; and that life should be free of pain. I had not grasped what "life on life's terms" really means. Even though I knew at some level that my challenges were an opportunity to learn valuable lessons, I was still trying to avoid pain, which is a very self-centered perspective from which to live—one which usually invites painful life lessons to help us shift beyond our own little world.

Just as we eventually saw that there was not a "spiritual side" to the program, that the entire program is spiritual, it is time that we recognize the same thing about life. There is not a "spiritual side" to life on our planet. Our challenges, our work and our play are all spiritual. Humanity as a whole must learn that there is no point where individual choices do not affect others. To believe otherwise is to maintain some form of denial that you are in fact responsible for and to your fellow man. The fellowships would not survive with this attitude, so how can we expect that the world will?

Moving Beyond the Status Quo

…some of us are faced with a crucial choice which dominates this entire incarnation: what are we willing to settle for? Are we willing to settle for peace of mind and affluence, or is the soul insisting on reaching toward mastery?

—JOHN RANDOLPH PRICE, THE SUPERBEINGS

A SHIFT SEEMS TO BEGIN AT SOME POINT BETWEEN THREE AND seven years of recovery, depending on how thoroughly you have worked the 12 Steps and practiced the principles in your daily affairs. It is most commonly recognized when you begin to ask yourself, "Is this all there is?" You have reached the status quo for successful recovery. You have developed a career, are moving toward financial responsibility, are active in the fellowship, working with others, and learning to have healthier relationships. In general, you are finding a sense of balance and personal responsibility. However, something seems to be lacking. Many people who experience this phase suspect their growth has become stagnant and wonder if the 12 Steps are enough. At this point, some find what they feel is missing through organized religion, but many people stay with their groups for many more years, hoping that the program that took them this far will pull them through in the end.

This is the point where I see members begin to leave the various fellowships. What they may not recognize is the return of a spiritual yearning for something more. The hole in the gut becomes noticeable again. Many members throw themselves into service work, or go back to the basics and work the Steps again, which is always a good idea. The basics will always keep you grounded in recovery. But rarely does the program completely provide the inspiration and support that is needed to take the member to his or her next stage of spiritual growth. The fellowship alone was never meant to provide for all of our spiritual needs.

Somehow, the status quo for full recovery began to be measured by employment, emotional stability, the length of time in recovery and contentedness. Many of us believed that we would be happy if we had these qualities, but eventually found they failed to provide the level of fulfillment we really desired. Sure, we want these things, but don't you also want to know that "the most satisfactory years of your existence lie ahead"? *(Alcoholics Anonymous)* If so, then we must be willing to take drastic action when necessary. Just as we were open to new ideas when we found the fellowship, we must continue to be willing to embrace new ideas as they are presented to us. These ideas surface from your own consciousness, from the collective wisdom that extends far beyond the knowledge you have gathered throughout your lifetime.

The desire for "something more" keeps returning because it is trying to lead you somewhere. We continue to cycle through feelings of restlessness, irritability and discontent for a valid reason. For some people in recovery, merely abstaining from pathological behavior is enough. For most people, it is not. In my work with people who have attained years of recovery, at some point they come up against an internal barrier. They are dealing with the subconscious or unconscious and the tools learned in 12 Step programs are not sufficient to go beyond the barrier. Even though this barrier prevents them from really achieving the life they dream of, many are unwilling to seek the outside counsel usually necessary to move beyond it. While the barrier is different for everyone, it tends to arise in areas that most of us deal with on a daily basis: faith, money, relationships, sex, emotions, and self-esteem. These issues reveal the deeply held yet faulty beliefs that are seeking illumination. Moving through this barrier requires a shift in consciousness and a renewed deep commitment to self-examination and remaining on a spiritual path. It is your opportunity to become more authentic and move beyond the status quo.

As a recovering person, you recognize that you must be diligent about the ongoing need for self-examination, walking through your fears and taking risks. Growing spiritually is something that you have committed to for the rest of your life. Your soul has chosen this path for a reason. You have surely seen people who chose not to grow spiritually and the consequences of this choice. Addictions return for a reason. We see people every day who swap one addiction for another, usually those that are perceived to be more acceptable, such as food, work or spending. When you see a new addiction forming in your life, it is present to move you beyond the status quo. The deep yearning that returns time and again is your soul seeking expression. I urge you to see this as a blessing and another sign that you do have an important role to play in the healing of our world—a role that your soul continues to remind you of when it gives you the choice to either be authentic or escape into a new addiction.

This spiritual hunger offers an opportunity for transformation for yourself as well as the world. In *The Way,* Michael Berg states that the Kabbalah teaches that the "highest level of striving is for transformation—for turning the desire to receive for ourselves alone into the desire to receive for the purpose of sharing." Many of us have survived extreme negativity in active addiction and continuously battle self-centeredness, which is nothing more than the desire to receive for the self, alone. Berg explains that we bring more Light into this world by continuing to overcome our self-centeredness. He goes on to point out that it is the action taken that opposes the desire to receive for the self, which actually amplifies the Light. One of the hidden blessings of addiction is revealed in his explanation that "the greater our desire to receive for the self alone, the more potential we have for revealing the Light—because if we change, if we succeed in transforming our nature, our past negativity transforms as well. The more negative our actions have been, the more Light that comes to be revealed." This concept allows us to begin to grasp the spiritual potential held in our recovery when we transcend the ultimate self-centeredness. Transformation will occur when illumination is brought to the darkness of our society.

Raising the standard of successful recovery means that we must redefine our power. This does not refer to the source of your power, but how you choose to use the power that is so freely given to you. Dr. Hawkins, in his book *Power vs. Force,* states, "The only way to enhance one's power in this world is by increasing one's integrity, understanding and capacity for compassion." It is only by grace that we have the gift of recovery. How we use this gift is our offering to society. With all the blessings we receive on a daily basis, surely we are to use this power to do more than create a comfortable life for ourselves. By moving beyond our complacency about what is going on in our community and our world, we share this gift and move into a new dimension of recovery.

It is time that we, as a society, relinquish the victim consciousness that has formed a breeding ground for apathy and powerlessness. It is amazing how many people feel powerless over social and political issues, regardless of how these issues impact their quality of life. Yet the same guiding force that allows us to be of service within the fellowship provides us with the power to be a vital part of the democratic process. If we are to truly move into a space where we are of maximum service, then we must be willing to accept total responsibility for our society—not just the present and future, but the past as well. We must be willing to look again at the choices we have made throughout our lives, in recovery and in active addiction, however good or not so good they were. It is the Fourth and Fifth Steps through a new perspective.

Being responsible for your own reality is not about changing your thinking to visualize the things you want in your life. It is about recognizing your life lessons, as well as how you energetically attract situations to help you gain clarity. It is about recognizing the power you possess and how your choices and beliefs manifest in your life. Carolyn Myss, in her incredible tape series, *Energy Anatomy,* explains it best when she says that you must look at how you create your own reality from an energetic standpoint, rather than from your personality. Most of us have spent years trying to get our thoughts in alignment with our desired goals so that we could create the reality we want, when it is our energy that we need to learn to manage. We can do all the affirmations in the world and it still may not help us master a lesson that our soul has taken on in this lifetime, especially if we are attempting to change only from the ego perspective or the personality. The ego perceives every-thing from a selfish perspective. Using affirmations without ad-ditional supportive practices is like trying to convince the ego to work with you. The ego may go along with the affirmation, but not let it penetrate to the subconscious. Or we may see the challenge, but not relate it to the bigger picture of our life les-sons. It is only through raising our own personal consciousness that we will be able to move beyond the ego perspective.

Many times, we get so caught up in our day-to-day chal-lenges that we establish a holding pattern before we start to ask ourselves, "What is the lesson here?" A common example of how we do this is seen the story of Jonah and Isabelle, recov-ering individuals who are parents of two young children. Jo-nah was in an automobile accident which totaled his car and left him unable to work for several months. He had no dis-ability insurance and minimal sick pay. Isabelle was a home-maker with no income. Until Jonah could return to work, the stress on the family just to stay afloat was tremendous. It was compounded by the fact that they had purchased a home they could barely afford and used credit cards to furnish the home. They were making car payments on two vehicles. To make matters worse, they lived off their credit cards while Jonah was recuperating. Even after Jonah returned to work, his inju-ries did not heal properly, so he continued to take time off for doctor's appointments. For years, the couple struggled to meet their financial obligations, barely getting by. They made no serious changes to their lifestyle or their pattern of spending. Like many parents, they wanted their children to have all the opportunities they had missed, so their expenses increased as the children became older. They lived from paycheck to paycheck, constantly juggling bills. Resentment grew between Jonah and Isabelle. The financial stress caused serious problems in the relationship, but they were determined to get through it by themselves. They waited seven years before they sought professional counseling for their personal and financial challenges. Seven years! Why wait until you are sinking to ask for help? That is certainly not what we have been taught in the fellowships, but this example is by no means atypical.

What are the lessons here? How could we look at this situation from a higher perspective? It is easy to see how one might get caught up in this situation. Nothing gets our attention more quickly than a situation that threatens our security. While we should never discount the importance of being financially responsible, there is a deeper lesson here. Do Jonah and Isabelle know what their values are? Does their behavior reflect these values? Is their personal ambition or desire for status, power and money diminishing their values? Are they looking for their security in material things? And what about their priorities in life? Is it our priority in recovery to achieve a middle or upper socioeconomic status, or is our priority to be a productive member of society? Asking yourself these questions (before life forces you to) will help you see the spiritual lessons inherent in any situation. Integrating the solutions into your everyday life will move you beyond the status quo of successful recovery.

Our lessons go so much deeper than the psychological or subconscious level. For instance, look at your family of origin. Did your soul choose this family, with its particular challenges? If so, what purpose have the challenges served toward molding your character and how have these challenges prepared you for being of service?

As you begin to look at soul lessons, you would benefit from finding someone trained in existential issues or transpersonal psychology. This is where you begin to heal the information that affects you without your conscious awareness. The unconscious is a realm that has received minimal exploration because it does not fit in with traditional psychology. For some reason, our society has come to a point that we need science to verify something before we give it credibility. While it may stretch your belief system to explore energy work or transpersonal psychology, would you prefer to continue to live in the problem? For those of you who have struggled to work through a particular issue for years without relief, the results will speak for themselves.

Your ability to participate in creating the world that you want, a world where extraordinary love, respect and compassion are the standard, depends on your willingness to move beyond your limiting beliefs. An understanding and awareness of our interconnectedness is too complex for the mind to grasp in one experience. While you may have deep and profound experiences which offer tremendous insight into this area, sustaining this realization is a completely different matter. It requires a conscious effort. Remember, your ego has an investment in helping you forget the truths that you learn. This is one of the reasons it is so important that we hear the same thing over and over in the meetings, to remind us of basic key points. Likewise, life is constantly offering us opportunities to gain a deeper understanding of our life's purpose and our personal lessons. Each experience of life provides us with another piece of the puzzle.

A trend in the fellowships indicates that people are achieving quality recovery more quickly than they did in the eighties and early nineties. This is indicative of the evolution of spiritual awareness which is occurring in our society. The deep spiritual work that so many people are doing right now is assisting all of mankind on their spiritual path, much in the same way that the world feels the benefits of organized and focused prayer. When individuals and groups make a commitment to a specific cause that benefits the earth or our society as a whole, tremendous healing occurs en mass rather than just individually. Moving beyond the status quo strengthens our role in this process.

Within the Fellowship

You cannot escape the responsibility
of tomorrow by evading it today.

—ABRAHAM LINCOLN

IF WE ARE TO BEGIN TO SPEAK OUT, EXPECT ACCOUNTABILITY
and become more responsible for creating the future we want,
we must begin within the fellowship itself. We initially test
our skills in the fellowship before taking them into the world,
so it is natural that the fellowship is where we would begin to
be proactive and look at what is best for all concerned. Twelve
Step programs are designed so that they can only be destroyed
from within. The 12 Traditions shield the fellowship from outside influence and provide a structure that outlines how the
fellowships should operate. Beyond these guidelines, it is the
members' responsibility to maintain the singleness of purpose
and compliance with the 12 Traditions.

The reason 12 Step programs are so effective in overcoming addiction is that they offer a simple spiritual solution.
Through the development of a relationship with the God
of our understanding, the 12 Steps provide a foundation for
learning to live with integrity, free from active addiction. Each
person in recovery has paid a huge price for this freedom. Just

as we cannot afford to take it for granted, nor can we afford to allow our fear and our denial to undermine our foundation. We must always be willing to look closely at whether we are upholding the spirit of our founding principles.

Our choices should sincerely reflect that the newcomer is the most important person in the room. As a rule, the fellowships are supportive of the newcomer as they struggle to find a God of their understanding. Members encourage the newcomer to use the group, or even a paper cup, as the God of their understanding until the newcomer is able to clarify a higher concept. But the suggestions are usually limited by the beliefs of those making the suggestions. Look at your own group and ask yourself, "Is this group truly respectful and comfortable with members sharing a wide variety of spiritual beliefs?" Are you open to members talking about their experience with healers, angels or energy work, for instance? Do you hear meaningful contributions about karma, spirit guides, reincarnation, a Higher Self, or the soul in meetings? My experience has been that we do not.

Members of the fellowship are most comfortable with a variation of God that resembles the Christian faith. While there is nothing wrong with this, if it is what the individual chooses, many individuals choose a concept that more closely resembles the Native American philosophy, Eastern tradition or the Jewish faith. These members are definitely in the meetings. Have you considered why we rarely hear their perspective? There appears to be a covert censorship occurring in the fellowships that involves the shaping of the individual's understanding of God. This is not some organized plan, nor do I believe that it is the intention of the members to undermine our founding principles. However, if we continue to limit members' beliefs to spiritual concepts that are primarily aligned with organized religion, then we are slowly sabotaging the effectiveness of our primary purpose.

Organized religion did not work for the majority of people in 12 Step programs—its constraints were too narrow for many of us to live by. The ability to develop the God of our own understanding provides us free reign in developing a spiritual life with practical applications. If the general interpretation of God as we understand him becomes the Christian philosophy, then we are imposing the same limitations on the fellowships, maybe with a slightly broader interpretation, that organized religion imposed on us. This is a dangerous position for the fellowships.

Throughout America, it is common to recite the Lord's Prayer during the opening or closing of a meeting. The Lord's Prayer is clearly a Christian prayer. How many times do you hear meetings close with a Jewish prayer? Never. Members would not stand for it. The World Service Office of the respective fellowships has no opinion on this because they do not dictate how the groups operate. They merely make suggestions. They are not going to tell the groups to stop using the

Lord's Prayer or micromanage them in any way. It is the local group's responsibility to ensure that our core principles are maintained, which means these issues must be addressed at the group level rather than at the world level. So, is your group upholding its responsibility? Or are you operating from fear that members might stray too far beyond your comfort level?

When we don't behave in a manner that is consistent with our stated values, it usually reflects a fear-based decision. Many newer members do not want to challenge the status quo or the seasoned members of the group. Others feel they are exercising their right to the God of their understanding when they do things like use the Lord's Prayer. I go back to question how these same members would feel if someone decided to close the meeting with a Hebrew or Native American prayer. There is nothing to say that it can't be done. We just haven't seen anyone do it yet. Justifications can be made for both sides of any argument, therefore we must be cautious about our personal feelings. We must vigilantly watch for the need to be right or to control too strongly. There is a much larger and more important issue here. The important question is whether the choices of each group reflect the founding principles, for it is the purity of these principles that allow the fellowships to be so effective for millions of people.

We teach newcomers that as long as their comments are confined to their experience, strength and hope, then they are free to share whatever they choose. However, my experience in meetings has been that speaking too openly about spiritual beliefs that directly conflict with the Christian philosophy results in negative social consequences. Personally, the expansion of my spiritual beliefs involved an exploration of the spiritual realm, the Native American tradition, Kabbalah and Eastern philosophy. I sought out shamans, energy workers and healers to assist me on my path. While it enhanced my recovery incredibly, it was not information that I was allowed to bring back into the groups without serious social consequences. I realize that the fellowships are not social organizations, but the reality for many newcomers is that the fellowship is their entire life. I understand that this is the norm for how society maintains conformity. But that should not be the case in 12 Step programs. The acceptance and encouragement of a variety of spiritual beliefs is what makes 12 Step programs effective for such a diverse group of people with various pathological behaviors. It is this core principle that makes these programs the miracle that they are.

An example from my own experience in early recovery reflects a challenge many may feel. A dear woman from the fellowship, who has remained a central figure on my spiritual path, introduced me to the study of metaphysics and a variety of philosophies that are ancient, deeply spiritual traditions in their respective cultures. She taught me to discern what was right for me and to recognize authenticity in the individuals I sought out. I will always be grateful to her for the patience and guidance she gave me. However, I began to experience the negative consequences from the fellowship immediately. As soon as I entered this new path, my sponsor dropped me. Those whom I thought were my recovering friends began to gossip about me, saying ridiculous things like, "She's worshipping the devil" and "She's going to use." Now, please understand that I had not stopped going to meetings, working the steps or taking any of the other actions that supported my recovery. I had simply added other aspects to my spiritual life, aspects the others did not understand and which therefore frightened them. I became the center of gossip within my rather large support group. At that point, I was still extremely sensitive and deeply in need of my support system.

I learned very quickly the limits about what was appropriate to share within the recovering community. What was professed by some to be unconditional love and tolerance for developing our own concept of God went only so far. I had the choice to conform or risk losing the support of the group. I truly believed that I needed these people to survive, so, of course, I chose to conform. Looking back, I see where I chose not to challenge the mores within the fellowship, as well as the community in which I lived. I gave up my authenticity to be a part of the group. I was still trying to fit in, only this time it was not among society, but the 12 Step fellowships. It may have been a good decision at the time, since I was able to maintain my recovery. But I also wonder if my spiritual development would have progressed more rapidly if I had not been so concerned about hiding my beliefs, or if my interests had been openly nurtured.

We have enough of a challenge finding support in the outside world; we should not be condoning this in the fellowship. In order to recover, we need the love, acceptance and community provided by the fellowship. Why would we want to limit support for each other or discourage someone from experiencing the fullest expression of their authenticity? When we confine the sharing that is allowed in meetings to less than the scope of the founding fathers' intentions, we have moved into a self-destructive pattern. This will slowly but surely diminish the strength of the fellowships.

Do we really want to place newcomers in this position? If the newcomer heard a sincere respect for diverse spiritual concepts, would more of them find recovery sooner? Would the fellowships be less likely to be perceived as a cult? Would more members with long-term sobriety remain active in the fellowship? If the field were wide open for a discussion of spiritual beliefs, would the entire fellowship evolve even more rapidly? Chances are good that the fellowship had a huge impact on your initial concept of the God of your understanding. We need to give newcomers the broadest possible opportunity to find the spiritual path that will work best for them.

The fellowships became the miracle that they are today by allowing the group conscience to be directed by a Higher Power. The fellowships will continue to evolve. If we resist change by trying to control too strongly, then we are not allowing room for a Higher Power to work. We have to find the balance of allowing the evolution to occur within the guidelines of the 12 Traditions. The responsibility for doing this will fall upon the members with mature sobriety who are better able to see life from a higher perspective.

We must always remember that our goal is to be of maximum service, wherever that leads us. It is a common belief in the fellowship that members should remain active in order to ensure their recovery. It is easy to see how this assumption developed. However, it may in fact be another belief that limits our usefulness to society. Being of maximum service to God and our fellow man may mean that the majority of the members with long-term recovery are supposed to leave the fellowships, to give back within the community. While there are many individuals whose purpose in life is to maintain the integrity and the very existence of the fellowships, many of us are needed elsewhere in our society. Whatever your role, 12 Step fellowships are preparing you be a part of the healing of our world—physically, emotionally and spiritually.

The fellowships discourage members from leaving, out of fear that they will return to active addiction. However, this is not a good reason to stay if you are certain that you are firmly grounded in recovery. Our best decisions are rarely made from fear, resentment, or any space of negativity. Ask yourself these questions. Can you truly maintain your commitment to service and living a spiritual way of life outside the fellowship? Can you maintain a faith that is fundamental to your life and evident in your behavior? The initial answer may be yes, but make sure this is not your ego talking. Even if you have a strong spiritually-based support system in place, very few support systems have the features that a 12 Step fellowship provides. If you strongly feel that leaving the fellowship is right for you, then try it. But be aware of symptoms that indicate you may not be prepared yet to live without this support system. Those symptoms include, but are certainly not limited to: an increase in self-centeredness; diminished standards for honesty; a primary focus on personal wants; less commitment to daily spiritual practices; more reliance on yourself rather than a Higher Power; a reduced focus on being of service to others; or the emergence of pathological behavior that can lead to another addiction. If you find these symptoms creeping back into your life, allow yourself the flexibility to return to the meetings.

Once a solid foundation in recovery is established, attendance of meetings is not about ensuring that you will no longer return to active addiction. It is about being there for others and being constantly reminded of the spiritual solutions that keep you grounded in your recovery. Assuming that you have learned to take what you can use and leave the rest, attending meetings is like having your spiritual batteries recharged. You may not see anything happening, but the power is certainly there.

If our fears prevent us from upholding the spirit of what our founders intended, we are undermining our existence, as well as the core concepts that make the fellowships so successful. Making it acceptable to look at recovery from different perspectives and with a higher purpose is a risk we owe ourselves as well as the future addicts who will need the fellowship. This is about so much more than the existence of the fellowships. This is about the existence of millions of people, as well as the well being of our world.

Let me state once again that I am not talking about changing 12 Step fellowships or the Traditions. I am suggesting that you go beyond your fears, within your group and your community, to ask yourself some challenging questions. I understand that the newcomer is the most important person in the room and the need for them to grasp 12 Step recovery in its purest form is vital. I also understand the fear that the 12 Steps will become diluted if we are not careful. I recognize that we are talking about human lives here. Should we not be just as concerned that the purity of the founding principles be preserved and taught to the newcomer? These are all complicated issues and I don't pretend to have all of the answers. I am suggesting that the newcomer might benefit from a broadened potential for what a life in recovery can hold. Hopefully, this book will open a dialogue for the recovering community to do some soul searching, not just about the status quo of recovery, but also about the direction of many of the groups.

3
PREPARING
FOR
OUR ROLE

Whatever task God is calling us to,

if it is yours it is mine, and if it is mine it is yours.

We must do it together—or be cast aside together.

—HOWARD HEWLETT CLARK,
ANGLICAN ARCHBISHOP OF RUPERT'S LAND

MY OWN SPIRITUAL PATH HAS GIVEN ME THE OPPORTUNITY TO experience a broad range of spiritual practices and to meet some incredible teachers whose messages are being widely received—messages about our inherent Divinity and about living consciously, about what it means to be a person of faith, the rapid evolution that is occurring in our world and the roles that we individually play in transforming our world. These messages are feeding the hunger of people who are searching for their calling in life, for their role in creating the world we would like to live in.

Many threads go into making a beautiful tapestry; no one thread creates the beauty by itself. Likewise, the role of every individual, regardless of their position in life, is important to the consciousness, the beauty and the degree of compassion in our world. We all have a purpose; there is no such thing as a life without significance. It is crucial that our society recognize the importance of *each* role that individuals contribute when they serve our community, whether they are collecting garbage, cleaning our schools or serving as an elected official. Every role is crucial, not just to our daily existence, but also to the foundation of the spiritual evolution of our community. Not only can we each bring a sense of dignity to our respective roles, we can bring a spiritual energy to whatever we are doing. We can express our appreciation of those who provide service in an honorable way.

Many recovering individuals are already in positions of leadership in our schools, in corporations and in government. We can be part of the foundation for change by recognizing the power that we hold, using it for the well being of our society and supporting others who are working to create positive change. The challenge for each of us is to become a *clear* channel of love so we are able to intuit guidance about how we can best be of service. This means we must always be willing to release the emotional baggage that prevents us from tapping into and expressing the Divine love that is within us, to move beyond the current status quo.

We know the basics—that life is a spiritual journey, that the Divine Presence is always with us, that we can't screw up too badly, that we all need each other. Now it is time to take the basics to a higher perspective—to see life energetically and symbolically. If life is truly a spiritual journey, then every event, every moment is a spiritual experience. There is significance in all things. Sometimes we get caught up in the big decisions of life and tend to give them more weight than the smaller decisions of our day-to-day lives, when it is really our day-to-day lives that reveal our level of consciousness. It is our interactions with each other that reveal our love and compassion. It is the choices we make when no one is around that reveal the degree of our dedication to a spiritual way of life.

We need to always be willing to move beyond our comfort zones. Adopting a broader perspective requires a willingness to expand our beliefs as we seek a deeper understanding of the interconnectedness of all living things. The steps teach us to readily admit when we are wrong, but if we can't even question our beliefs, then we are locked in with no room for authentic growth. Continuously exploring and expanding our understanding of life helps us to develop more love and compassion, which is vital to spiritual growth.

There is a common ground where all spiritual beliefs can coexist. Isn't it our responsibility to share this truth within our respective communities? It takes courage to be visible with your spiritual beliefs, especially when they directly conflict with people you hold dear in your life. I am not suggesting we attempt to convince anyone of anything, or that we proudly proclaim our spiritual beliefs. However, if we truly believe in a spiritual principle, such as the right to individual spiritual beliefs, then it should be open for discussion when we see this principle violated, whether it is in our home group, our community or the government. Becoming visible in the fellowship or at a civic level is a huge risk that many of us have avoided for a long time. If we all keep waiting for someone else to approach the tough topics, such as respect and tolerance of spiritual and cultural differences, civil rights or accountability, then our progress towards peace for the human race will be extremely slow.

I invite you to shift your perspective to encompass the bigger picture, to see how all of life is supporting your spiritual growth, how your consciousness affects those around you and contributes to our world as it exists. I am talking about learning to live consciously, about exploring the reason for your existence and how you attract into your life situations which help you reach your full potential. What is the purpose of your challenges, and how do they relate to your being of service? What are the challenges of our society trying to teach us? As with all 12 Step programs, our first step is to consciously admit that we do not have the answers to the unmanageability that we are living with. Once we become willing to truly follow our path and be open to guidance and answers, they come to us.

In order to take your recovery to the next level, a spiritual plane that you have probably had glimpses of, you will have to be honest with yourself like never before. Life will present you with the opportunity to see aspects of yourself that you may not have been capable of acknowledging before. For many people, it will require an evaluation and possible reorganization of their priorities. Are you ready to be clear about all the ways you are dishonest with yourself? Are you ready to accept responsibility for creating everything that happens in your life? Are you ready to be more responsible in your community? Frankly, it is much easier to say that you are not responsible for what is going on in your life or in this world than it is to accept responsibility for creating the life you want. This is known as victim consciousness, and our society is plagued by it.

The greatest gift you can give yourself is to make the decision to live consciously, recognizing how the events of your life have been preparing you for the new dimension you are entering. And it is a new dimension—one supported by your willingness to commit to your fellow man. It is important that you are totally committed to being of service, because life will immediately begin to present you with situations that speed up your clearing process. Remember, recovery is an inside job. Your life is an outward expression of your thoughts, beliefs, emotions and your Spirit—essentially, your consciousness. Emotional baggage of the past will surface for you to release it. All the ways in which you reflect a victim consciousness will be revealed so you can accept complete responsibility for the life you have created. Your soul came into this lifetime to experience certain lessons and themes; like it or not, you are creating the circumstances in your life for your soul to master these lessons.

Life gives us constant clues as to the direction we should on take our individual journeys. Just as living a life of recovery took time to master, so will looking at life through this new perspective. Learning to live in the flow of life takes practice and commitment. Our challenge now is to embrace this responsibility and commit to walking our spiritual paths, whatever that entails. I used to feel that my spiritual evolution began when I came into recovery. Today, I know that it began long before that. The experiences of both my childhood and active addiction were simply setting the stage for the woman recovery has helped me become. I know that everything in this world is interconnected and that while the God of my understanding speaks directly to me, just as he does to everyone, this Presence also communicates through the people, places and situations that I encounter on a daily basis. Looking at life from an energetic perspective is the same as looking at life from a spiritual perspective.

Recovery is about spiritual *growth*. I am talking about a spiritual commitment that far exceeds the status quo for most fellowships. We frequently hear people who have become content in their recovery say, "At least I haven't lost what I had." But if we maintain the current status quo, is this true? Most of us attained this level of recovery through passion, commitment and a willingness to go to any lengths, not by being content. Maintenance and growth are completely different. Twelve Step programs have always stressed that we are either moving forward or backward, that there is no such thing as standing still. We can only truly exercise our God-given power if we continue to expand and challenge what *we* have established as the status quo.

Be open to looking at your addiction, your recovery and your role in society. Allow yourself to move to a higher perspective and to openly consider what that role might be. Not only do I believe there is a reason our society is plagued with addiction, I suggest that rather than being a hindrance to society, it is serving as a stepping-stone in the spiritual evolution of our world. In order to actively participate in a constructive way, the recovering community must take a more active role in accepting responsibility for creating the world we want, in the same way that we honor and protect the 12 Step fellowships and our recovery. It is time that we acknowledge, through our behavior and our choices, that our second chance in life leaves us with a responsibility far greater than ensuring that the fellowships exist for the next generation.

If you have made the decision to develop to your highest potential, then expect events and people in your life to give you a push that forces you to learn to stand outside of convention. This preparation process involves the reorganization of priorities. You must develop the capacity to follow your spiritual path, wherever it takes you, regardless of how far fetched it may seem by those closest to you. Once again, the challenge of fitting in arises, as well as the fear of ending up alone and judged as being crazy. Remember that there are many individuals like you who are working to build the courage to follow their path. You will always attract people into your life who support your authenticity. You will also recognize at an even deeper level that success, measured by external standards, lacks meaning. Just as living with integrity is something that you do for yourself, so is fulfilling your spiritual purpose something that you do simply because you must.

Lead by Example

The hope of a secure and livable world lies
with disciplined nonconformists who are dedicated
to justice, peace and brotherhood.

—MARTIN LUTHER KING, JR.

WHAT DOES A SPIRITUAL PERSON LOOK LIKE? A LOT LIKE YOU and me, your neighbor, co-worker or friend. They have challenges to walk through, an ego to overcome and moments when their faith wavers. Our society sometimes acts as if we have a shortage of role models, but do we really have a shortage, or have we too narrowly defined the stereotype of what a role model should be? People are often hesitant to be perceived as a role model because of the spotlight and expectations that often comes with the role. When we think about a role model, we often think about this squeaky clean, good guy/gal who is as honest as the day is long, has no relationship challenges, is generous with their time, talents and money, gainfully employed, usually middle class or higher, always helping others… you know the rest. This ideal contributes to the irrational belief held by the majority of our society that, to some degree, they are not good enough. Good enough by whose standard?

What about the person who has made every mistake possible and still succeeds in turning his or her life around? The person who continues to face their challenges with as much dignity and courage as they can, who sometimes falls short of their stated ideals, but acknowledges and atones for their shortcomings? The man or woman who continues striving to be their best with the character flaws they may have, and positively contributes to the community, regardless of their socioeconomic status? Isn't this man or woman more representative of the average citizen? Isn't this a better ideal for us to support, rather than expecting people to live up to a standard that is virtually impossible?

As a society, we are starved for authenticity. One of the main reasons that the world has fallen in love with Oprah Winfrey is because she is real. We see her basic goodness; regardless of whatever challenges she has faced, most of the world loves Oprah. Would all of that change if she made a mistake tomorrow? I seriously doubt it, since her intrinsic goodness far outweighs any mistake she could possibly make. She has never tried to pretend that she is without challenges. We see her flaws and millions of people around the world love her anyway.

In movies, television shows and fiction, central characters often have significant shortcomings and flaws which conflict with their ideals. We witness their struggle to live by these ideals, however; it is in their redemption that we get so excited.

The same is true for you and everyone else. We should be celebrating each other's redemption, rather than passing judgment on each other's weaknesses. Your inherent goodness far outweighs any bad choices you have ever made.

I urge you to sit down and look at your priorities and your values—not in your head, but on paper. In your head, you will probably come up with a list of glorious qualities that you strive for in your life. On paper is where reality starts to sink in. Does your behavior reflect what you say your priorities and your values are? If not, you can expect to attract challenges to help you see any discrepancies and bring your behavior into alignment with your stated ideals.

Building integrity is crucial, not only to your spiritual way of life, but also to your success in becoming a visible presence in your community. You will not attain a sustained sense of fulfillment in recovery until you learn to live with integrity. People are always looking for ways to build their self-esteem, but are not sure exactly how to go about it. Self-esteem and integrity are really the same. However, behaving in a manner that builds integrity is more easily defined. If you allow yourself small indiscretions of dishonesty and think it is okay, you are deceiving yourself. If you do not honor your commitments just because something more appealing comes along and you think it doesn't matter, you are deceiving yourself. If you choose to ignore the challenges and crises that occur within your community, does this reflect integrity? It doesn't matter if everyone does it. These behaviors will not build integrity. Nor does it matter if no one else knows about your deceptive behavior. What matters is that you know about your behavior; this knowledge is what really undermines your self-confidence. Your self-esteem is a reflection of the respect that you hold for yourself. Living with true integrity is something that you do for yourself, not for others. The Steps provide an outline, not only for how to clear up the past, but for how to deal with situations in which we behave in a manner that is not consistent with our highest ideals.

We have to learn new levels of personal responsibility, healthy relationships and value-oriented living. These areas have traditionally been outside the scope of a sponsor's role, and rightly so. You see, many sponsors don't know much about these areas themselves and we all know that you can't pass on something that you do not have. If you have over ten years of recovery, the issue is severely compounded, since the number of people with more time than you is drastically low. So, where do you find mentors outside the program? If you are maturing in your recovery and ready to accept responsibility for your role in creating the world you would like to live in, then open your eyes and see who is around you. Remember the old saying, "When the student is ready, the teacher will appear." These teachers may be the people we least expect, but they will present themselves in our lives. Our challenge is to not place an expectation on what our teachers should look like, what religion they practice, or how they are dressed. Nor should we disregard our teachers because the lesson they are here to teach isn't the one we want to learn.

Be open to receive people into your life, but realize that there is a certain amount of fear you will be required to work through. A man who was very influential in my early recovery taught me how to grieve when another member of the fellowship passed away. Both of these men were considered by most of the group to be the "rock" upon which to lean during tough times. This wise man shared with me that when you lose your "rock," it is an indication that it is your turn to become the rock. It is your turn to become the mentor that models the new level of value-oriented living. It is your turn to teach, through example, how to live from a higher level of consciousness. The quality of your recovery will be directly proportionate to the extent that you are willing to embrace your role in this world.

With a history as self-centered as ours, we should never underestimate the challenge that living with true integrity presents. Integrity can be just as difficult to sustain as it was to attain, if you are not diligent. Life presents us with dozens of opportunities every day to allow small breaches in the wall of our integrity. Each time we allow ourselves the small indiscretion of going against our values or what we know is best for all concerned, we are contributing to a cumulative effect. If you are not careful, you may wake up one day and realize that your standards have been lowered to the point that you have to totally rebuild your foundation. If you find yourself at this point, be gentle with yourself. Living with the integrity that we strive for is a challenge. We are not perfect, nor are we ever going to be perfect. Rebuilding your foundation is simply the pruning process of life which allows you to shift your standards from average to exceptional. Inevitably, something very positive comes from this painful process, something that was necessary for you to reach your full life potential.

Some of you have made more progress than others when it comes to living with integrity. We have all seen those who are further along the path judge their peers who were experiencing challenges in order to learn this vital code of personal honor. We have probably been one of them at some point. There is no room for judgment on this path, especially considering we all have a past. Most people don't recognize that judgment is really a projection of their own self-perception, a defense mechanism used to externalize aspects, beliefs and qualities that are surfacing in your awareness, but not yet integrated. Our experience has taught us a degree of compassion that many who have not gone through active addiction will never know. Be grateful for where you are in your spiritual evolution, but never doubt that, without commitment to your path, you could very easily be in the other person's shoes. As the old saying goes, "…but for the Grace of God…."

Hopefully, you are already creating a more realistic role

model for your children and future generations. Instead of asking them to strive for perfection, you allow them to see how you honorably deal with choices which could result in negative consequences. By becoming visible and allowing the world to see the commonalities of a variety of spiritual beliefs, we can also contribute to the spiritual evolution that is occurring. We can become the role models our society needs in order to learn to be a more loving, tolerant and compassionate society.

The 12 Steps and 12 Traditions have given us many tools to use in modeling peaceful coexistence. They have taught us that our common welfare should come first; in fact, our personal recovery depends on this. Becoming a more productive member is, in part, our amends to society. However, simply being a productive member of society falls short of the spirit of amends. To be or do what we were always intended to be or do, does not atone for our behavior in active addiction. Our experience has taught us that a mere willingness to atone for our behavior will manifest the opportunities to do so.

So, what would it look like to make amends to society? We might begin by holding our elected officials accountable, writing them letters stating our position on specific topics, or attending city council meetings. It may mean that we become active in a local charity whose interests reflect our beliefs, or that we contribute in some way to a cause that is working to correct the environmental destruction occurring in our world. Whether it is something as simple as recycling or as challenging as saving our forests and rivers, there is a role for everyone. It definitely means that we wake up and become informed about what is going on in the world. It is not even necessary that we be right about a certain issue. Remember, being right is not the issue. There will always be opposing views, but both views need to be heard. It is how we identify the needs of all concerned in order to find a win-win solution.

A good example of this can be seen at the World Service Conferences held by the major fellowships. Members of the fellowships, serving as delegates from throughout the world, come together to discuss and make decisions about the future of the fellowships and the challenges they are facing. Although only delegates are allowed to vote on motions presented at the Conference, generally anyone is allowed to attend. It is an educational experience, one that can help you see more clearly how to transfer the skills exhibited here into most situations in your community. At one of the World Service Conferences, a motion was introduced on an issue, and then hotly debated for hours, as many issues are. A vote was called on the motion, and the majority of the Conference voted in favor of it. After the motion passed, however, one of the delegates requested that she be allowed to make a minority statement about the issue. After hearing the minority opinion, many of the delegates who had voted in favor of the motion recognized the importance of the minority opinion and took the proper steps, through Parliamentary Procedure, to reconsider the issue. After more hours of debate, the Conference members realized that the minority opinion was in the best interest of the fellowship as a whole. The original motion was rescinded and a motion was made that supported the minority opinion. It passed overwhelmingly. While this is a lengthy and exhausting process, it is a beautiful example of how open-minded individuals who are willing to explore all views come together and make decisions for the sake of a society. Although personalities may arise throughout the Conference, the presence of a Higher Power guiding the process is clearly present.

We live in a democratic society. We play a role in the way we operate, the choices we make and the things we choose to ignore. I am challenging the individuals in the recovering community to up the ante, to participate at a higher level. If even a fraction of the recovering individuals in this world decided to be seen and heard, we could be talking about a million people worldwide.

So, where do you begin to lead by example? The first step is to shift your perspective to a higher consciousness. Your life will reveal the specifics for you. You must, however, make a commitment to stop living small, to stop holding yourself back from fear of what others will think, say or do. We have to give each other permission to move beyond the status quo, to be brilliant, empowered and creative. You possess unique qualities and abilities that only you can bring to this world; they were there in active addiction, just as they are in recovery. You simply have access to a much higher power in recovery.

We must carry the lessons of the fellowships into the world with the same love we show the newcomer, for it was love and a spiritual awakening that transformed each of us personally and it will be love and a spiritual awakening that will transform our world.

Embracing the Challenge

Experience is a hard teacher because she
gives the test first, the lesson afterwards.

—VERNON SANDERS LAW

Learn your lessons quickly and move on.

—EILEEN CADDY

LIVING ON A SPIRITUAL BASIS DOES NOT MEAN THAT YOU WON'T
have challenges. Each challenge has the potential to bring us
clarity or to further muddy the issue, depending on our perspective. Our challenges serve many purposes, all of which
prepare us for our role in helping to transform our world.
They are here to reveal a deeper understanding of life—one
that is necessary for our continued spiritual growth.

Our challenges are blessings in disguise. A dear friend of
mine taught me that "our challenges do not mold our character; they reveal our character." They reveal the wounds that
still need to be healed and the beliefs that keep us in bondage
to the ego. Often, they lead us to our greatest teachers—those
whose role is to help us integrate spiritual laws into a deeper
understanding of the true meaning of life.

When you wrote your Fourth Step, you probably saw several life patterns of self-defeating behavior. The purpose of the Fourth Step is to clarify the causes and conditions that set these patterns of self-destruction into action. As you grow to higher levels of consciousness, life will present you with challenges to take the insights gained in the Fourth Step to even deeper levels of understanding. Your ability to conceptualize and integrate lessons during your first year in recovery is limited by the many changes that are occurring within your body and your mind. Although significant spiritual growth occurs, most of your energy is focused on simply maintaining abstinence. Early in recovery, your challenges present you with opportunities to reinforce your commitment to recovery by choosing abstinence over active addiction. Once abstinence has become a way of life, your challenges help you develop a deeper understanding of how your character defects are blocking your spiritual connection. They always reveal the lessons most important to your spiritual growth.

Maturing in recovery is about continuing to move beyond your self-centeredness and to grow in service. In early recovery, individuals are taught to move beyond the craving to use by turning their attention to situations in which they can be of service. Working with others allows you to return to your own circumstances with a more grounded and less selfish perspective. At this stage, while addicts have made great progress in reducing their self-centeredness, they tend to still spend the majority of time thinking about themselves, how situations affect them or whether their needs will be met. Indeed, we often need to be reminded that our needs are consistently met. It is our wants that the ego is preoccupied with; it is the ego we are working to transcend as we remain on our spiritual path.

The tendency to look superficially at the circumstances of challenges ensures that a similar challenge will occur. If personal growth is not a high priority and you are satisfied with the status quo, you may choose to deal only with the current conflict. Perhaps you recognize the wisdom of avoiding the same situation. Your denial, however, may prevent you from recognizing the deeper meaning hidden within the challenge. Your soul is always seeking a higher expression. Those who are immersed in their spiritual growth may encounter many of the same challenges, yet be able to see how the challenge relates to the bigger picture. Challenges serve to deepen our understanding of the interconnectedness of life and how one experience builds on another. Those who are committed to their spiritual growth and have adapted a broader perspective will understand that the situation is not some cruel testing, but a tender preparation for being of ultimate service.

Let me give you an example of the levels of learning held at different points in recovery. Adam had a pattern of dating women who were overly dependent on him. Over a twelve-year period, he had three significant relationships, each of which lasted more than two years. Adam usually held the role of being the more responsible member of the relationship. The relationships never appeared to begin so unbalanced. In the beginning, his girlfriends seemed to be independent, attentive to his interests and needs, financially responsible and committed to their personal recovery. While each of his girlfriends had substantial incomes, they also seemed to spend excessively for their own interests, with minimal concern for building a solid financial future. Adam always insisted his girlfriends move in with him. Eventually, he would grow resentful of the imbalance within the relationship and the relationship would begin to deteriorate. With each relationship, Adam was able to gain deeper insights into the lessons held in each challenge.

In the first relationship, Adam did everything he could to pamper his girlfriend and reassure himself that she needed him. Because neither knew how to communicate effectively, their conversations remained superficial. The more he did for her, the less she seemed to appreciate him. Adam finally reached the point of feeling totally taken for granted when his girlfriend quit her job and made the decision to go back to school without having first discussed it with him. She had no family to provide financial support while she pursued her education and had assumed that Adam would continue to support her. After leaving the relationship, Adam recognized how his feelings of being unlovable placed him in a position to have to buy his girlfriend's love and attention. Initially, he identified himself as a victim, but eventually saw how he had placed himself in a position to be used. He also recognized that his need for someone, anyone, to be there for him was preventing him from learning to be comfortable with himself. It was a huge step in developing his self-worth. By recognizing his own strengths and valuing himself, he was able to differentiate between spending on his partner because he wanted to and spending because he felt the need to buy her love.

With each ensuing relationship, Adam learned to communicate his wants and needs a little more clearly. In his second relationship, he clarified his expectation that the bills were to be split equally. However, he still did the cooking and cleaning. He catered to his girlfriend's wants, and tried to predict and fulfill her every need. He listened to her financial, career and personal challenges, always offering support. He planned and paid for trips which reflected her interests more than his own. He felt more appreciated, but was not yet in a mutually supportive relationship. Toward the end of this relationship, Adam was able to realize that, at some level, he was recreating his parents' marriage. He realized that his relationships reflected many of his parents' same patterns. Just as he, as a child, had sought his mother's attention through whatever means necessary, he did the same with his girlfriend. After leaving this relationship, he was forced to explore his issues surrounding his parents at a much deeper level; he realized how many of the traits he found unattractive in his father were present in his own life. Adam had to also look at the unfulfilled needs from his relationship with his mother and realize how he was seeking to fulfill those needs through his girlfriends.

In the third relationship, Adam had learned to reach compromises with issues such as expenses, household chores and recreational activities. He was clear that a relationship built on healthy interdependency was important to him. Adam's spiritual path opened new doors for him and his hunger for spiritual growth intensified. He extended his service work beyond the fellowship and became involved with a group that mentored youth, an activity which he found fulfilling. His girlfriend, however, continued to struggle with personal issues. Her interests had changed over the years and her lack of commitment to her career was evident in her failure to advance within the company. As time went on, she grew more depressed and fearful of a career change, unable to see the destructiveness of her self-centeredness. Adam was always there for support, making suggestions, encouraging her to find a mentor, and offering to help in any way that he could. It was only when he began his work in transpersonal psychology that he recognized his soul lessons at an even deeper level. From a higher perspective, he was able to recognize how he attracted partners who allowed him to be in control and supported his false sense of personal power.

Adam is a compassionate person, perceived by himself and others to be confident and independent. Being the person that people turned to when they were looking for answers provided him with a sense of power. Through the energy exchange that occurs within all interactions, Adam was essentially usurping others' power in order to maintain his own. Relying on another person's energy to bolster your own actually victimizes the other person. In his book, *The Celestine Prophecy,* James Redfield provides a thorough explanation of the energy exchange which occurs between individuals. He describes a variety of "control dramas" that people tend to subconsciously and unconsciously use in their search for power. And what are we all searching for in life? Power. It is easy to see how Adam's deeper life lessons were being revealed to him over the years, as he gradually evolved to a higher consciousness. He moved to a deeper level of personal honesty and gained a respect for others. His new understanding of energy allowed him to view all of life differently and to access his power from within rather than through external sources.

According to John Randolph Price, our life lessons usually fall into one of four categories: relationships, money, career or health. The basic lessons are the same for all areas and the solution is always about improving our relationship with the God of our understanding. Challenges are present to help us become more compassionate, to develop trust not just in our fellow man but in the God of our understanding, to rely more on our spiritual power which will never fail us, to trust that we will be provided for if we follow our calling, and to recognize the interconnectedness and the presence of the Divine in all things. For instance, if your lessons surround money, it's not simply that you need to learn to be financially responsible. Your irresponsibility is present to help you gain clarity into a deeper lesson. It may be that you are searching for value and security through money, or learning to recognize your responsibility to care for your fellow man. The same lessons could be presented through illness, dissatisfaction in your career, or unhealthy relationships. These are simply the vehicles through which lessons manifest. Life presents us with opportunities to learn that personal value is not dependent on money, career, health or relationships. Our challenges are opportunities for those "ah ha" moments in which the pieces fall together perfectly.

Throughout life, you will be presented with countless opportunities to recognize your most pertinent lessons. Two of the most common lessons are held in the hallmarks of addiction—dishonesty and self-centeredness. Your struggle with honesty is life's way of teaching you the importance of integrity, as well as to trust on a higher level. Challenges surrounding self-centeredness help you become a more compassionate person and recognize the interconnectedness of all life.

When we fall short or face a challenge, we must continue to look for the spiritual lesson. Full awareness of what is really going on within you is very difficult. Denial is strong; our filters can be very dense and sometimes we simply are not yet prepared for a deeper understanding of what current events are preparing us for.

I am reminded of a statement made by Albert Einstein:

"You can't solve a problem with the same mind that created it." In essence, he was saying that we must allow our minds to shift to a higher consciousness in order to see the solutions to our current challenges.

A change in perspective would help us to see that 12 Step programs are preparing us for our role in the world, rather than creating a world for us to live in. Addiction is helping us find our spiritual foundation. When we shift the way we look at the problem, not only does the solution become evident, sometimes we see that there is not really a problem.

Living Consciously

Our heart glows, and secret unrest gnaws
at the root of our being...Dealing with the
unconscious has become a question of life for us.

—CARL JUNG

IN THE LAST FORTY YEARS, OUR SOCIETY HAS EXPERIENCED A gradual spiritual awakening. Largely outside of organized religion, we have begun to dedicate more time to our spiritual life, to seek spiritual guidance and growth, to recognize the interconnectedness of all life. The challenge now is be consciously aware, in each moment, that everything in life is spiritual.

To live consciously is to be present, aware and engaged in life's interactions, with the knowledge that whatever you are doing in any moment is *your purpose in life*—that your highest potential is indeed held within each breath. This moves you from doing, to being, and provides you the opportunity to access your intuitive abilities so you may recognize your highest potential. This is living consciously.

Consciousness is defined as "a sense of one's personal or collective identity." The depth of your consciousness is reflected in the material plane, in your everyday life. A dear friend and professional educator, Carol Lampman, strongly encourages the participants of her trainings to look at their challenges and ask themselves, "How is this like my life?" Whether it is about bumping into things, dealing with financial challenges or having a total meltdown on your computer, life is attempting to communicate with you. This communication is often metaphoric or symbolic. For instance, if you find yourself driving around, knowing you are lost but resistant to asking for directions, you might ask yourself if this is symbolic of your life. Are you moving through life with no clear direction about where you are going? Are you resistant to asking for help?

Living consciously means that you are focused on the people, the conversations and the situations of each moment. You acknowledge the bigger picture and recognize the interconnectedness of all things. You know that whatever harms your fellow man, at some level also harms you. You are aware of your feelings. You are not concerned with multitasking. You don't allow your mind to be in the past, the future, or on a different topic. You are in present time. Living consciously also means that you recognize that this moment is not an insignificant and isolated event, but a vivid thread of the tapestry of your life. It allows you to more easily see the Divine Presence at work in your life and identify the lessons your soul has attracted to move you to an even higher level of consciousness.

Just as a puzzle is put together one piece at a time, so

does each experience contribute to the richness of the overall beauty of life. But, as with any puzzle, you may pick up several pieces before you figure out where they fit or are able to see the beauty of the full picture. You may have to wait for another experience before you can see how your current experience is useful in your life. Living consciously frees you from the desire to make your life look like someone else's. It provides an understanding that we each bring a valuable contribution to this world.

In early recovery, most people begin to see "coincidences" happening in their lives—events which can be recognized as evidence of a Divine Power operating on the physical plane. It is an exhilarating feeling, but too often quickly dismissed. It happens time and again, yet we are always pleasantly surprised when it occurs, even a little amazed. When you live consciously, you realize that such synchronicity is constantly occurring. It is equally as exhilarating, but no longer surprising. It becomes a guide for your spirit and a constant connection to your inner joy. The God of your understanding is constantly communicating with you. Albert Gaulden, in his most recent book, *Signs and Wonders: Understanding the Language of God,* discusses many of the different ways that life is constantly affirming our highest ideals and guiding us to them.

While life isn't necessarily supposed to be free of difficulty, it also doesn't have to be a constant struggle. Lessons and challenges don't have to be as hard as we make them. As we learn to live consciously, more in the flow of life, our challenges don't have to beat us up before we finally understand the lesson. Many times, it is the smaller, more hidden experiences and choices that are the most powerful. Carolyn Myss reminds us that God usually appears in what seem to be small, humble packages. According to Michael Berg in *The Way,* the Kabbalah teaches that "what is subtle and undisclosed is always more powerful than what is explicit and fully revealed."

Living consciously means that you must learn to trust your intuition, to listen to that still small voice inside of you. It takes practice, especially for those of us who tend to be logical and practical, so be patient with yourself. That voice may take many forms. It is the part of you that acknowledges the coincidences. It may be a feeling that you need to call someone or do something outside of your normal routine. This is usually a brief thought that you may consider unimportant, if you are not careful. If you feel a resistance to following through on an impulse that is not logical, use this resistance to learn to recognize when you are having an intuitive thought. For instance, you may feel inclined to take a different route home, but your head starts to list all the reasons you should stick to your routine. The argument in your head is the cue that your intuition has surfaced. Even though it may cause a delay in arriving home, it also might facilitate a "chance" meeting with someone that you need to see or you may avoid an accident that occurred on your normal route home. You don't always need to understand the reason for the intuitive thought. It may arise to teach you to trust the process. Sometimes, we are simply exercising the ability in order to strengthen the skill. In responding to these intuitive thoughts, you will begin to recognize other intuitive skills, such as simply knowing something when you have no logical reason for knowing. Living consciously allows you to learn to recognize your own intuitive cues.

Learning to sense and read energy will also strengthen your ability to live consciously. Have you ever had the experience of walking into a room and immediately sensing that something was wrong? You were probably right. Throughout your recovery, you have probably relied on your ability to sense energy to avoid situations that would make you unsafe. The energy can be palpable in situations in which circumstances are jeopardizing your recovery.

Stop when you enter a room and allow yourself to feel the energy in the environment. Begin to pay attention to the way you feel around certain people and places, allowing yourself to sense the energy. Likewise, make sure that the energy you bring into any situation is positive. Our attitudes and our thoughts have a tremendous impact. They carry an energy that contributes to every situation we encounter. Quantum physics is proving that all things in life, in their very essence, are forms of energy which respond and react to each other. Notice the difference in the energy when you move the furniture around in your home, how certain colors "feel" better than others, how sometimes things are not in the "right" place. You rely on your intuitive ability to sense energy much more than you think.

Everything in this world is connected on an energetic level. Our bodies are constantly regenerating themselves; they function from an energy impulse emitted by the heart. Native Americans have recognized for centuries the energy that is inherent in all things. The earth, nature and the four directions are acknowledged in all sacred ceremonies of the Native Americans. When we see all things as part of the Divine and honor them as such, we operate more fully within the flow of life.

Living consciously and trusting your intuition requires that you learn to discern, especially between fear and intuition. Think of something that really frightens you and notice where fear is stored in your body. Allow yourself to really sense the energy of the fear. Now, get in touch with your intuition. Think of a time when you "had a hunch"—when you simply knew something. Notice the difference between your intuition and your fear. How are your body sensations different? Skepticism can be a good thing, just be careful that your skepticism isn't really your fear. Moving to a higher level of consciousness requires that we be willing to walk through our fears about concepts that may currently be outside of our current beliefs, both about our personal power and about life itself.

Becoming conscious in relationships requires that we look at the patterns of our relationships as they emerge. Recognizing the patterns that exist in each relationship gives us great insight into our life lessons. It often means that we have to be very honest about some unpleasant aspects of ourselves, like how we use people to maintain our own sense of power, or how we contribute, covertly or overtly, to the patterns and qualities that we dislike in our partners, family members and coworkers.

If your goal is to live consciously, with a stronger awareness of your soul's purpose, you must recognize that psychological tools will only take you so far. If addiction is truly a spiritual malady, it stands to reason that spiritual tools will be necessary for its treatment. The 12 Steps are the basis for solid recovery, however most fellowships recognize their limitations. Any thorough inventory will reveal subconscious beliefs manifesting in your behavior. Additional tools are necessary to allow members to move beyond the current status quo of recovery. These spiritual tools allow you to tap into your subconscious and unconscious thoughts, feelings and perceptions. Since they influence your life from a realm outside of your conscious awareness, it is crucial you find the appropriate tools to delve more deeply into these levels of consciousness. Tav Sparks describes a variety of these powerful tools or practices, many of which are non-traditional, in his book, *The Wide Open Door: The Twelve Steps, Spiritual Tradition and New Psychology.*

Bill Wilson, one of the cofounders of Alcoholics Anonymous, referred to us as being in a spiritual kindergarten. Moving to a higher perspective, working with the subconscious and the unconscious to reveal our soul lessons, may mean that we have moved to the first grade. It certainly indicates a thirst for learning more about universal consciousness and how it can be utilized to create a world that is beyond our imagination. It is time for society to learn to recognize and value spiritual guides and practices that will help us move to higher levels of spiritual growth.

Twelve Step recovery is simply our foundation—it is the framework that allowed us to reconnect to the Divine. To grow in recovery, we must continue to expand our spiritual life and embrace a deeper understanding of Spirit. If you have ever distanced yourself from people who wear crystals, participate in sweat lodges, talk about gurus, or chant, for instance, I encourage you to open your mind to new ideas and then, of course, take what you can use and leave the rest. This is where you truly embrace diversity and begin to create a new status quo, not just for the fellowship, but also for your community.

The Eleventh Step provides the foundation for living consciously by reinforcing the necessity of practicing daily prayer and meditation in order to improve your conscious contact with the God of your understanding. Prayer and meditation provide a ritual that, when practiced conscientiously, will reveal how life is constantly communicating with you, providing guidance for your path. While a few moments spent with a meditation book each morning may have sufficed in early recovery, it is not sufficient for developing higher states of consciousness. Meditation is a discipline that requires dedication and commitment. Pema Chodren emphasizes the importance of meditation for society as a whole in her book, *When Things Fall Apart.* She says, "If we really knew how unhappy it was making this whole planet that we all try to avoid pain and seek pleasure—how that was making us so miserable and cutting us off from our basic heart and our basic intelligence—then we would practice meditation as if our hair were on fire. We would practice as if a big snake had just landed in our lap. There wouldn't be any question of thinking we had a lot of time and we could do this later."

Our answers are always inside of us. Meditation allows us to access this information by going directly to the Source of our power. We will still need guidance from others—sponsors, mentors, families—to help us interpret and implement our intuitive cues. In living consciously, however, we recognize that we don't need anyone else to provide us with answers or tell us what is best for us. As we become more adept at recognizing and operating from our intuition, we rely less on others for validation. The standard for recovery becomes dramatically different when we consistently receive our direction from the Source about the actions we must take in transforming our world.

4

BRAVE
ACTION

&

A ship in the harbor is safe
but that is not what ships are for.

—JOHN A. SHED

THERE IS NO BETTER EXAMPLE OF COMMITMENT TO BRAVE action than the life of Martin Luther King, Jr. As one of the most visionary individuals of the twentieth century, Dr. King led the movement to ensure the civil rights of African Americans. Equally as important was his commitment to social change through nonviolent action. Dr. King's passion and commitment to a spiritual way of life were evident in his writings, his speeches and his actions. His belief in human rights, nonviolence and challenging the status quo of our government meant that he had to endure physical assaults, bomb threats, imprisonment, the death of loved ones and the ultimate sacrifice of his own life. He was never deterred by his own fear. His path would have been much easier had he not been so visible in evoking social change, but he recognized his role in transforming our world.

Becoming more involved in the transformation of our world requires brave action, passion and commitment. We must remember that Dr. King was simply the leader of the civil rights movement. He could never have done it alone; it took thousands of people committed to the cause of transformation to fulfill Dr. King's dream. Millions of recovering individuals can collectively be just as influential in the transformation of our world. Will there be consequences for attempting to create change? Naturally there will be, but hopefully they will be more positive than negative. There will most certainly be consequences if we fail to take action. Many of us have hesitated to step out there in order to prevent our past from being revealed. Our fears, as well as our desire for love and acceptance, have stood in the way of many opportunities to make a difference. Unfortunately, there will always be people who want to undermine you, or are jealous and critical. Some will be people that you thought were your friends. You cannot let them stop you from following your spiritual path. If you strive to operate from your most spiritual self, you will overcome these obstacles. We must remember that we are all human; not only will we make mistakes, we will sometimes fall short of our chosen ideals. Just as people won't always support us, at times we will disappoint our friends. If our common goal is to bring new meaning to being a productive member of society, then we must show each other the same compassion and love that we show the individual who has just relapsed. During these crucial periods of transition, we continue to support them. We love them anyway and we tell them that they are always welcomed. We honor their brave action and commitment to their spiritual path.

The only thing that can stop us from being more socially active and bringing the principles we live by to a more visible level is fear—fear of being wrong, of enduring the stigma attached to being an addict, of what other people will say, of having some aspect of our past surface, of inviting challenges into our life, of giving up what we have decided will create a safe, comfortable life. We will have challenges, and some of them will be unpleasant. Likewise, other learning experiences will be exciting and rewarding. Change is going to occur in our society, so we might as well make choices that we believe will make a positive influence. You do have the power within you to make things different. You have unlimited power if you are on a spiritual path.

A passage in Michael Berg's *The Way* closely resembles a passage in the book *Alcoholics Anonymous*. Berg states, "To the extent you choose, through positive action, to destabilize everyday reality, the Light will reward you with a new reality beyond anything that you might have expected." The Big Book states, "The things which came to us when we put ourselves in God's hand were better than anything we could have ever planned." Both passages refer to courageous action, to a total surrender and commitment to being used for the good of society as a whole. What specifically does it mean to destabilize everyday reality, to take brave action? It means that we individually find our specific areas in society to commit to service, that we remove the stigma of addiction and that we model the principles of the fellowship in a more visible way.

Beyond Anonymity

Life is either
a daring adventure
or nothing.

—Helen Keller

THE 12TH TRADITION STATES, "ANONYMITY IS THE SPIRITUAL foundation of all our traditions, ever reminding us to place principles before personalities." Anonymity serves many purposes. It is crucial for the protection of both the individual as well as the fellowship. Anonymity allows the newcomer to develop a strong foundation in recovery without risking the repercussions of society's bias against addicts. It also serves to protect the often spiritually arrogant member whose pride moves them to want to flaunt their recovery. Primarily, it protects the fellowships from the public perception that any single member who states that he or she is a member of a certain fellowship, represents the membership or the fellowship as a whole. Twelve Step fellowships have no representative beyond their World Service Boards. The breach of anonymity for less than honest motives has caused unforeseen pain to numerous members.

I believe that, as members of the fellowships, we have taken the concept of anonymity too far. The majority of the time, members don't know each other's last name, even within their home group. This is not what the founding members intended. Their intention was to protect the members and the fellowship from outside influence. In respect to anonymity, Dr. Bob said there are "two ways to break the anonymity Tradition: (1) by giving your name at the public level of press or radio; (2) by being so anonymous that you can't be reached by other drunks." At that time, stating that you were recovering or in a 12 Step fellowship automatically revealed an affiliation with AA. That is not true today. You can say that you are recovering without mentioning a specific fellowship and it is anyone's guess which one you are talking about. Disclosing that you are a recovering person, even at the media level, is not a violation of the Traditions *as long as you don't indicate affiliation with a particular fellowship or break someone else's anonymity.*

At times, the 12 Step fellowships remind me of the secret societies and mystery schools that taught their members ancient spiritual practices—how to live with integrity, commit to service for their fellow man, and fulfill a spiritual role within society. Their knowledge was thought to be esoteric in nature and only for a few chosen individuals. The difference is that 12 Step fellowships are for the masses.

Twelve Step fellowships are preparing individuals across the globe for a higher purpose by teaching us these same values. We have been given priceless tools. We know that to maintain harsh emotions toward other groups or individuals can lead to nothing but further destruction, perhaps even our own. We have learned that the answer to all problems is held in further spiritual development.

It is time to publicly take these tools to a more visible level. If you have achieved solid long-term sobriety, then I encourage you to ask yourself whether you need to maintain your anonymity about your recovery. If your answer is "yes," can you clearly identify why? Most reasons for maintaining anonymity will fall into one of the categories that we are most qualified to change: the bias that society holds against addicts and alcoholics, or the complacency that exists once the status quo of successful recovery is achieved.

There comes a point in your recovery when breaching individual anonymity allows you to be of greater service than maintaining it. Most of society doesn't realize that we are everywhere in our communities, because, for the most part, we have become productive members of society and are thus more invisible because we don't fit the stereotype of the alcoholic or addicted person.

A potent example of this was seen in *The West Wing,* a popular television show which aired an episode in which the President found out, after many years, that his Vice President was a recovering alcoholic. In the episode, the fellowship worked just as it should have in protecting his anonymity. But was anonymity taken too far, and for what purpose? Should we allow those who are closest to us, even those we work with, know we are in recovery? Would our society elect a president or vice president if they acknowledged they were recovering alcoholics or addicts? Probably not, but our history indicates that we will elect active or untreated addicts. There is something seriously wrong with this picture. Once again, the only reason for maintaining anonymity so tightly is the potential social implication of the stigma. The reality is that there are countless numbers of us in positions of significance. We are in these positions for a reason. But are we too anonymous?

Is shifting the public's perception of addiction part of our responsibility to those who are still suffering? Everyone would certainly benefit from removing the stigma of addiction. If this is part of our role in creating change in our society, can we realistically do this without breaking our anonymity? Because of the stigma attached to addiction, my personal code for breaking my anonymity was on a need-to-know basis. But if we all hold this code, the stigma of addiction will continue to exist. Instead of seeing both sides of the issue—active addiction and recovery—we let the world see active addiction, and then live in recovery behind the cloak of anonymity.

At some point, your recovery will serve a higher purpose through breaking your anonymity than through maintaining it. I challenge you to ask yourself if you are there now. We are at a perfect junction in our society to let our presence be known in order to shift the perception of addiction. I am not suggesting that you go out and promote the fact that you are recovering. I am suggesting that you allow those with whom you interact the most frequently know that you are in recovery. More and more, I acknowledge my recovery when I am getting to know someone, simply as an aspect of who I am. Many times, I still feel that twinge of fear just before I disclose my recovery. However, I have committed to taking the risk that comes with doing this—and it is a risk. It is a small step, but we all know that major change begins with small steps.

Search your soul to make sure that the reason you are disclosing your recovery is not solely self-serving. There may be situations in which this choice backfires on us while trying to shift the public's understanding of addiction. Suppose that a recovering person decides to run for public office and discloses that they are recovering. Will their past be made public? Probably. Should this issue stop the individual who has an important contribution to make to the community? I hope not. This is just one of the many scenarios in which creating a paradigm shift through moving beyond the stigma of addiction will require courage and tremendous support. My hope is that the recovering community will support the individuals who choose this ground breaking transition as they move beyond anonymity.

Removing the Stigma

The most important thing is
to be whatever you are
without shame.

—Rod Steiger

WE CAN NO LONGER ALLOW THE STIGMA OUR SOCIETY HAS placed on addiction to continue as it is. It does not serve anyone. I talk a lot about change in this book for two reasons. One is to remind you that change is going to occur, regardless of whether we become more proactive. The second reason is because change must occur for us to create the type of world we want to live in. The risks involved in becoming proactive in our society can be great, but so are the potential rewards. If you have resonated with anything in this book, perhaps you are being called to be a part of the social change that our society so drastically needs. Addictions are our teachers in this lifetime and, frankly, I could think of a lot worse teachers to have. We, who are so intimate with addiction and recovery, can help shift the current perspective of addiction more effectively than anyone else.

The stigma that our society holds against addiction should be something that we take personally. We, more than anyone, have a vested interest in eliminating the stigma of addiction. As a society, it sabotages the essence of what recovery is working to achieve and perpetuates the stereotype. Instead of supporting recovery, holding this stereotype forces individuals and families to continue to hide while the addiction escalates. The stigma often remains, even when we have been in recovery for many years. Often, newcomers place this stereotype on members with long-term recovery. Women that I work with sometimes need to hear my story to grasp that at one point I really was in their shoes.

This stigma holds serious implications and continues to place recovering individuals in precarious situations. Addicts continue to be discriminated against by the medical community, insurance companies and employers. If you are recovering and not insured through a group insurance plan, chances are slim that your application for coverage will be approved. Despite the fact that it is commonly recognized as a disease, insurance companies rarely treat alcoholism as they do other medical conditions. When they do agree to provide treatment, it is minimal and on their terms, regardless of the individual's needs.

We are definitely treated differently by physicians and medical professionals. Medical professionals frequently perceive all somatic complaints by addicts as drug-seeking behavior. I have personally had the experience of being denied pain medication after surgery. Because the surgery resulted in pain for weeks afterward, medication would have been prescribed to anyone else. I doubt that my experience is unusual in any way; we've all had these experiences. These are just a few of the everyday occurrences that we face—situations that we must begin to confront and to change.

Have you ever struggled with the decision about whether to be honest on an employment application when it asks about drug treatment, or former arrests or convictions? While we know that we must answer honestly, because lying on the application is grounds for immediate termination, we are keenly aware that answering "yes" may mean the employer never allows an interview. Have you chosen not to reveal your recovery at work because of the potential for being treated differently? How many times have you been excluded from social or business occasions on the pretense of not wanting you to be uncomfortable? (Who is really uncomfortable?) If the stigma were not so common and deeply entrenched, we would not have these dilemmas.

And let's not forget our families—the stigma extends to them as well. A friend with over eighteen years in recovery recently shared that she did not break her anonymity because she feared the parents of her daughter's friends might not understand. She was attempting to shield her six-year-old daughter from the ramifications of the stigma. This is a woman who volunteers for her daughter's school, the local museums and other social causes. Those of you in Alanon, Naranon, Coanon, ACOA, or other groups for family and friends of the addicted, understand the shame associated with addiction as well as anyone. Children and parents of the addicted often end up having as many emotional challenges as the addict. Parents feel they have failed in some way when their children are addicted; children hide their family member's addiction from their friends. Recovering individuals who are parents will often experience the stigma of addiction from both perspectives, as their children face their own addictions.

If addiction were not perceived to be such an immoral weakness, would more individuals with food addiction seek help? Obesity in America indicates that there are probably as many individuals addicted to food as there are individuals addicted to both legal and illegal drugs. People are buying millions of books in search of a solution. And just as many of us tried to control our use or adapt our behavior, overeaters are attempting to deal with the issue of food. Food is just a symptom of the issue, but most of society is not aware of this. How can we create a more receptive social climate for them to face their challenges? As a group, we have the power to create anything we want.

Many in the recovering community are already looking for remedies to the discrimination that is so prevalent. A recent article on a recovery website encouraged litigation when dealing with discrimination. While this may be appropriate in some circumstances, I feel we can find more effective ways to deal with discrimination. When we individually use the tools we are so familiar with, the appropriate actions become clear. If those of us who are the target of discrimination, who know that there are two sides to addiction, are not willing to address the issue, then what does that say about us as responsible citizens? How can this not be an aspect of being of service to the still-suffering addict? I don't know many people who are willing to take on these issues by themselves, and you really can't blame them. However, we can't sit back and pretend that this is not our challenge to deal with.

We can only begin to implement solutions to removing the stigma of addiction by becoming more visible and proactive in our community. Would our society benefit from seeing how many respected citizens are in recovery? In the long run, it probably would. We have to look for solutions that offer a win/win solution and appeal to a higher level of consciousness for all involved—our employers, our family members and members of our communities.

Becoming Proactive in Our Communities

Do the thing and you will have the Power.
—Ralph Waldo Emerson

Be realistic: Plan for a miracle.
—Bhagwan Shree Rajneesh

MANY OF THE SOCIAL ISSUES THAT WE FACE TODAY—HOME-lessness, AIDS, domestic abuse, child abuse, hunger, poverty, murder, theft and other forms of crime—have a direct correlation with addiction. They are challenges that affect everyone. Our health care and judicial systems are overwhelmed with the consequences of addiction. Our prisons are filled beyond capacity because of drug-related crimes. For years, we have heard about the war on drugs, but we never seem to make much progress, most likely because it is a war we cannot win based on our current strategy. Our government spends billions of dollars annually on addiction and related social issues. Whose money do you think we are spending? It's our money, of course. Don't get me wrong—these areas have to be addressed, but we know better than anyone else that treating the symptoms of addiction is not an effective solution. It creates an endless spiral further into addiction.

The longer we delay in looking at the underlying causes and conditions of addiction in our society, the worse things will become. Who is going to spearhead the challenge of looking at the causes and conditions that perpetuate the cycle of addiction? Will we as a society leave it for our children or grandchildren to deal with? If so, are we preparing them to deal with these issues through education and mentoring of spiritual principles, or are we simply acting as if the white elephant is not in the picture again? Surely, the recovering community is not going to pretend that we don't know the solution. While we may not know exactly what actions to take, we know the Steps necessary to find them. We know how to access the guidance and direction that will be required. Putting the solution into place, however, will require that we become much more active at a social level.

Who is better prepared to confront these social issues than those of us with a solid foundation in recovery? Exactly how you do this will be an individual decision, but on some level you already know where your contribution will be. What issues do you find yourself complaining about or are you the most frustrated by? What issues do you feel the most passionately about? For some, it will be children, the elderly, or animal rights. Others may be more passionate about politics, the environment or health care. Have you dreamed of doing something that would make a positive contribution to our society, but allowed your past to stop you? Remember, it is time to relinquish the victim consciousness. Recognize that these ideas are present in your mind for a reason. They are your soul seeking greater expression. Take the risk to do extraordinary things.

Consider yourself a source of spiritual energy in every moment of your daily life. Be a source of love. Allow yourself to approach all situations, even those that frustrate you, with love and a vision of peace. The love we encountered when we entered the rooms of the fellowship had the power to transform us. The quality of this love comes from the soul. This love held the space for us to do the deep work that was necessary for recovery to occur. The same power that helped us to heal individually will also help our communities to heal.

We owe it to future generations to do more to change the direction of our society. It is within the last century that we so drastically began to abuse the earth, that we placed such a strong emphasis on possessions and money as determinants of status, that we chose to deal with the epidemic of addiction by incarcerating the addicted and treating the symptoms of this social disease. It has been in our lifetime that we have developed the medical and technological abilities to save so many lives around the world and then have not found a means to make it happen. We have contributed, either covertly or overtly, to the challenges our society faces today; it is therefore our responsibility to address the issues.

We lived through the Cold War and the destabilization of Russia, experienced the rise in terrorism and are witnessing the escalation of conflict throughout the world. We live in a volatile world. History will look back at this point in time as a crucial period that marked a turning point for our world. If we want to maintain the level of comfort and freedom that currently exists, we have to get involved. Violence is not the answer. Locking people up is not the answer. Pretending we are powerless over the situation is not the answer. We need to implement spiritual solutions more than ever. Whether we call this a crusade, a new perspective or just being a productive member of society does not matter, as long as we take action.

5
BECOMING THE
PERSON YOU ARE
MEANT TO BE

Our deepest fear is not that we are inadequate.
Our deepest fear is that we are powerful beyond measure.
It is our light, not our darkness, that most frightens us.
We ask ourselves, who am I to be brilliant, gorgeous,
talented, fabulous? Actually, who are you not to be?
You are a child of God. Your playing small doesn't serve
the world. There is nothing enlightened about shrinking
so that other people won't feel insecure around you.
We are all meant to shine, as children do. And as we let
our own light shine, we unconsciously give other people
permission to do the same. As we're liberated from our
own fear, our presence automatically liberates others.

—MARIANNE WILLIAMSON

Transforming our world sounds like a tall order. If you recall, recovering from your addiction appeared to be just as impossible. Much depends on you and your willingness to be of service in the highest capacity. One thing is for sure—a total commitment to being of service will be required.

We are a group whose every move is stalked by rebellion. Don't be surprised if your initial response to these ideas is conflicted. There is nothing in what I have suggested that conflicts with the underlying principles of the fellowships. Your first reaction may be from your ego, which is always looking for the "easier, softer way"—the way of saying nothing, doing nothing. By now, you also know that what appears to be the easier way rarely is. The 12 Step fellowships are preparing us to play a significant role in transforming our world. Actively participating will require that you move beyond your current level of comfort, your fears and your denial.

Now is the time for us to step up to the plate in numbers, adopting the same commitment to the human race that we hold for our respective fellowships. It is time that we take the underlying principles that make 12 Step recovery so effective into our communities, and do so in a humble, yet visible way. While society has never looked at the addicted as a group with tremendous power, we know differently. As members of this group, we know how powerful we can be when we allow our actions to be guided by a Higher Power.

We must be willing to examine and release our restrictive beliefs, to move beyond the fears for our personal security as well as the fellowship. A Higher Power is in charge of both. We have to stop trying to fit in and learn to be comfortable with our role in life. It is not our job to fit in. It is our job to be constantly moving to a higher level of consciousness. We must develop the capacity to follow our inner guidance, even when that means we have to take on difficult challenges. We have to look at recovery from a higher perspective than we are accustomed to, to move beyond the status quo of successful recovery. You can be a part of raising the standard.

In the chapter "A Vision for You," the early members of AA wrote, "God will show us how to create the fellowship we crave..." and "the most satisfactory years of your existence lie ahead." While recovery has blessed us greatly, these statements continue to reflect the future that is available to us if we live by spiritual principles. By embracing our challenges and living consciously, we gain the ability to adopt a broader vision of the meaning of life. Seeing life from an energetic perspective allows us to utilize all of our intuitive skills. It enhances the spiritual foundation that 12 Step recovery has provided. Living consciously means that you start where you are in this exact moment and allow yourself to become the person you are meant to be.

As I write this book, I am constantly examining my life to see where I am living the ideas I am proposing. As with most people, some days I do better than others. My strength lies in the fact that I know what kind of woman I choose to be. I choose to make a difference in my little corner of the world. I choose to exercise not just my right, but also my responsibility, to be a part of the democracy of my country, the direction it takes and its responsibility to care for our environment. I choose to talk about the white elephant standing in our local, state, and federal buildings. I choose to acknowledge, support and empower the people in my community. I choose to respect myself enough to be kind when I fall short of my goals and to see these moments as opportunities to learn vital lessons. I choose to live passionately, to take great risks and to receive great rewards. And I choose to deeply love and be loved. I choose to do all of this from the highest consciousness I am able to achieve. I invite you to join me in this commitment. We will make a difference.

Ask and it shall be given you;

seek, and ye shall find;

knock and it shall be opened unto you.

For every one that asketh, receiveth;

and he that seeketh, findeth;

and to him that knocketh,

it shall be opened.

—MATTHEW *7:7–8*

REFERENCES

ALCOHOLICS ANONYMOUS, Third Edition, (1976). New York: Alcoholics Anonymous World Services, Inc., pp. 25, 100, 152, 164.

Berg, Michael, (2001). THE WAY, New York: John Wiley & Sons

Bhagwan Shree Rajneesh, Rajneesh Foundation International

Caddy, Eileen, (1979). THE DAWN OF CHANGE, Findhorn Press

Chodren, Pema, (2002). WHEN THINGS FALL APART, Boston: Shambhala

DR. BOB AND THE GOOD OLDTIMERS, (1980). New York: Alcoholics Anonymous World Services, Inc., p. 264

Gaulden, Albert (2003). SIGNS AND WONDERS: UNDERSTANDING THE LANGUAGE OF GOD, New York: Atria Books

Hawkins, David, M.D., Ph.D., (1998). POWER VS. FORCE: THE HIDDEN DETERMINANTS OF HUMAN BEHAVIOR, Sedona, AZ: Veritas Publishing

Jung, Carl, *Time Magazine*, 14 February, 1955

King, Martin Luther, Jr., (1986). THE STRENGTH TO LOVE, Minneapolis, MN: Fortress Press

Myss, Caroline, (1996). *Energy Anatomy,* Sounds True Audio

Price, John Randolph, (1997). THE SUPERBEINGS: OVERCOMING LIMITATIONS THROUGH THE POWER OF THE MIND, Carlsbad, CA: Hay House

Redfield, James, (1994). THE CELESTINE PROPHECY, New York: Warner Books

Sparks, Tav, (1993). THE WIDE OPEN DOOR: THE TWELVE STEPS, SPIRITUAL TRADITION AND NEW PSYCHOLOGY, Center City, MN: Hazelden

Williamson, Marianne, (1992). A RETURN TO LOVE: REFLECTIONS ON THE PRINCIPLES OF A COURSE IN MIRACLES, New York: HarperPerennial

THE 12 STEPS

1   We admitted we were powerless over alcohol—that our lives had become unmanageable.

2   Came to believe that a power greater than ourselves could restore us to sanity.

3   Made a decision to turn our will and our lives over to the care of God as we understood Him.

4   Made a searching and fearless moral inventory of ourselves.

5   Admitted to God, to ourselves, and to another human being the exact nature of our wrongs.

6   Were entirely ready to have God remove all these defects of character.

7   Humbly asked Him to remove our shortcomings.

8   Made a list of all persons we had harmed, and became willing to make amends to them all.

9   Made direct amends to such people wherever possible, except when to do so would injure them or others.

10   Continued to take personal inventory and when we were wrong, promptly admitted it.

11   Sought though prayer and meditation to improve our conscious contact with God as we understood Him, praying only for knowledge of His will for us and the power to carry that out.

12   Having had a spiritual awakening as the result of these steps, we tried to carry this message to alcoholics and to practice these principles in all our affairs.

THE 12 TRADITIONS

1 Our common welfare should come first; personal recovery depends upon A.A. unity.

2 For our group purpose there is but one ultimate authority—a loving God as He may express Himself in our group conscience. Our leaders are but trusted servants; they do not govern.

3 The only requirement for A.A. membership is a desire to stop drinking.

4 Each group should be autonomous except in matters affecting other groups or A.A. as a whole.

5 Each group has but one primary purpose—to carry its message to the alcoholic who still suffers.

6 An A.A. group ought never endorse, finance or lend the A.A. name to any related facility or outside enterprise, lest problems of money, property and prestige divert us from our primary purpose.

7 Every A.A. group ought to be fully self-supporting, declining outside contributions.

8 Alcoholics Anonymous should remain forever non-professional, but our service centers may employ special workers.

9 A.A., as such, ought never be organized; but we may create service boards or committees directly responsible to those they serve.

10 Alcoholics Anonymous has no opinion on outside issues; hence the A.A. name ought never be drawn into public controversy.

11 Our public relations policy is based on attraction rather than promotion; we need always maintain personal anonymity at the level of press, radio and films.

12 Anonymity is the spiritual foundation of all our traditions, ever reminding us to place principles before personalities.

ABOUT THE AUTHOR

TAMMY PEACOCK MEGAHEE, LCSW, has been recovering and working in the addictions and mental health field for 17 years, developing innovative programming, facilitating weekend workshops, and hosting THE HUMAN POTENTIAL SERIES, a motivational lecture series featuring nationally prominent authors committed to the evolution of our society. As a counselor and educator, she maintains a private counseling practice specializing in nontraditional therapy techniques and serves as an adjunct faculty member in the Social Work department at Miles College in Birmingham, AL. Tammy is currently pursuing a Ph.D. at the University of Texas at Austin.

Give the Gift of
BEYOND ANONYMITY:
A COMMITMENT TO A HIGHER CONSCIOUSNESS
to your family, friends and colleagues.

Order here or visit www.BeyondAnonymity.com

❏ Yes, I want_____ copies of BEYOND ANONYMITY for $14 each.

❏ Yes, I am interested in having Tammy Peacock MeGahee speak at an event I am planning. Please contact me.

❏ Yes, I would like to be included on your mailing list for newsletters, events and announcements of future publications.

SHIPPING/HANDLING $3.95/book; $1.50/each additional book.
Alabama residents include 8% sales tax.
(Canadian and international orders, please refer to the website.)

Payment must accompany orders.
My check or money order for $_____ is enclosed.
Please charge my ❏ VISA ❏ MasterCard

Name _____

Address _____

City/State/Zip_____

Phone _____ Email _____

Card #_____ Exp. Date_____

Signature _____

Make your check payable and return to:
TRUETT ENTERPRISES PRESS
P. O. BOX 550160
BIRMINGHAM, AL 35255-0160

www.BeyondAnonymity.com
205/933-9777

NOTES

NOTES

NOTES